PLANNING FOR THE PAST

Volume 2

An assessment of archaeological assessments 1982–91

PLANNING FOR THE PAST

Volume 2

An assessment of archaeological assessment procedures in England 1982–91

by Timothy Darvill, Stephen Burrow, and Deborah-Anne Wildgust

BOURNEMOUTH UNIVERSITY

ENGLISH HERITAGE

1995

First published 1995 Bournemouth University

Copyright © Bournemouth University, Talbot
Campus, Fern Barrow, Poole, Dorset BH12 5BB 1995

A catalogue record for this book is available from the
British Library

ISBN 1 85899 003 3

English Heritage Product Code XC10702

Edited by Kate Macdonald and Ellen McAdam
Edited and brought to press by David M Jones
Designed by Typografica and Anne Jenner

Printed in Great Britain by
Whitstable Litho Printers Ltd., Whitstable, Kent.

Contents

List of figures

List of tables

Preface

Desk-based archaeological assessment and field evaluation of development sites has become a familiar exercise over the past decade or so, and in 1990 was endorsed by the Department of the Environment in Planning Policy Guidance note 16 (PPG 16) *Archaeology and planning*. Not all early examples of what we might now call desk-based assessments or field evaluations were carried out as systematically or as rigorously as they are today. Collectively, however, the experience that has been accumulated around the country has brought to archaeological resource management a set of approaches and methodologies which goes a long way towards providing the basic information that curators of the resource need in order to take informed views about the preservation, conservation, and management of archaeological remains.

Much effort and many resources have been devoted to carrying out desk-based assessment and field evaluation over the last decade. With the certainty that such work will continue in the future, it is important to review the successes and achievements of what has been done so that archaeologists working in all sectors of the profession can benefit from the increased understanding of the process itself and the knowledge that has derived from it. This need appears all the greater when it is realised that the scale of archaeological assessment has increased despite a general downturn in the economy. As the property development industry gains momentum after the recession of the early 1990s the number of assessment exercises carried out is likely to increase dramatically.

The work to date has raised important academic, methodological, and practical questions. Among these are the degree of consistency in the application of desk-based assessment and field evaluation procedures in different parts of the country, what is done with the information derived from these projects, how the findings of such work can be integrated with data from other sources to enhance the growing body of archaeological knowledge, and how other archaeologists can find out what has been done.

English Heritage, as a national body charged with the curation of the archaeological resource, considers that the most effective way to ensure that the processes of desk-based assessment and field evaluation fulfil expectations within the archaeological profession and beyond is to review current practice periodically. This is the first such national review of assessment procedures.

The review is based on a systematic survey of archaeological contractors and curators carrying out desk-based assessments and field evaluations between 1982 and 1991. The results are reported in two parts. This volume contains a documentary and analytical study of assessment practice over the last decade in England. The second part is a consolidated directory of recorded archaeological desk-based assessments, field evaluation reports, and the archaeological components of environmental statements which have been made available to the researchers working on the project (Darvill *et al* 1994). The research project on which this review is based was undertaken for English Heritage by a research team working under the direction of Professor Timothy Darvill in the Department of Conservation Sciences at Bournemouth University.

In parallel with this national review, a detailed study of the application and efficacy of field evaluation procedures in the counties of Hampshire and Berkshire was carried out under the direction of Drs Timothy Champion and Stephen Shennan of the Department of Archaeology at Southampton University (Champion *et al* 1995). The report on that project is complementary to this review, and the two should be read in conjunction.

This review identifies a number of areas where improvements could be made in the future development of desk-based assessment and field evaluation procedures, their relationship to professional practice, and more effective promulgation of the results of such work. Recommendations resulting from the Assessment of Assessments study as a whole are being issued separately by English Heritage (English Heritage 1995).

T C Darvill
Bournemouth
October 1994

Acknowledgements

The authors are extremely grateful to all those organisations and individuals who responded to the questionnaires and requests for information about past and present projects, and all those who generously gave of their time to explain the strengths, weaknesses, and opportunities presented by assessment projects known to them. The Assessment of Assessments project was executed and monitored with the help of a steering group drawn from different sections of the archaeological profession. We would especially like to thank the members of the group for their advice and comments at all stages in the evolution of the project: Geoffrey Wainwright, Stephen Trow, and John Hinchliffe (English Heritage); Timothy Champion, Stephen Shennan, and Paul Cuming (University of Southampton); Paul Chadwick (Lawson-Price); Andrew Sargent (Royal Commission on the Historical Monuments of England); and David Buckley (Essex County Council) and Mike Hughes (Hampshire County Council), successively representing the Association of County Archaeological Officers. Sir Peregrine Rhodes and Mr William Walker of the British Property Federation kindly supplied useful comments on the draft project design.

Much of the work for the pilot study at the beginning of the project focused on Cornwall, Devon, and Somerset, and for their patience and helpful suggestions while being constantly pestered for different information we would like to thank Nick Johnson and Steve Hartgroves (Cornwall), Simon Timms and Frances Griffith (Devon), and Bob Croft (Somerset). In the later stages of data gathering, contact was made with archaeologists and others in many parts of the country; grateful thanks are extended to all those organisations and individuals who helped assemble and collect data for the project even when at first sight the task seemed awesome. The Appendices to this report list all those organisations which were contacted and whose efforts contributed to the work of the project. Analysis of environmental assessment programmes was greatly facilitated by the kind assistance of staff at the Institute of Environmental Assessment, especially Julie Tarling and Martin Slater.

Hilary Williams developed the databases for the project, undertook the pilot studies, and started the main programme of data collection before her tragic death in a road accident while *en route* to the IFA Conference in April 1992. Since July 1992 the project team consisted of Deborah-Anne Wildgust and Stephen Burrow, assisted for a short period by Jonathan Roberts. Assistance from Bryan Brown (Head of Department), John Beavis and Fred Wildgust (computing), Bob Fletcher (administration), and Anne Gifford, Lindsay Drew, and Pamela Mackenzie (secretarial), all of the Department of Conservation Sciences at Bournemouth University, is gratefully acknowledged. Thanks are also due to everyone with whom members of the project team had informal discussions about assessment procedures and methods and who read and commented on drafts of this report, especially the following: Bill Startin, Graham Fairclough, and John Schofield (English Heritage); Nicola King, John Wood, and Alan Hunt (Bournemouth University); Susan Davies and Andrew Lawson (Wessex Archaeology, Salisbury); Neil Holbrook and Graeme Walker (Cotswold Archaeological Trust, Cirencester); and Christopher Gerrard (King Alfred's College, Winchester).

Abbreviations

ACAO Association of County Archaeological Officers
CBA Council for British Archaeology
DoE Department of the Environment
EC European Community
ES Environmental Statement
EH English Heritage (Historic Buildings and Monuments Commission for England)
GIS Geographical Information Systems
HMSO Her Majesty's Stationery Office
IAM Inspectorate of Ancient Monuments
IEA Institute of Environmental Assessment
IFA Institute of Field Archaeologists
MAFF Ministry of Agriculture, Food, and Fisheries

MSC Manpower Services Commission
NAR National Archaeological Record
NERC National Environmental Research Council
NMR National Monuments Record
PPG Planning Policy Guidance (issued by the DoE)
RCHME Royal Commission on the Historical Monuments of England
SAM Scheduled Ancient Monument
SBAC Science-Based Archaeology Committee (of the National Environmental Research Council)
SI Statutory Instrument
SMR Sites and Monuments Record
UK United Kingdom

1 Introduction

Background

Determining the nature, extent, quality, and importance of archaeological remains is a difficult business, particularly since the necessary data are often buried below the ground. In archaeological resource management, however, such information is needed for many reasons, most notably when professional judgements have to be made about the desirability of preservation or the establishment of conservation and management programmes in the face of development pressure. Throughout this report the term 'development' is taken to mean property development in its broadest sense: the enhancement of land values through the execution of capital works and the regeneration of land, buildings, and infrastructure. It includes city-centre commercial development, residential and industrial development, recreational and leisure-based development, the construction of new roads and services, and certain elements of estate management, agriculture, and forestry. As a process, the accumulation, sifting, and assimilation of data relevant to the formulation of professional judgements may be termed 'assessment', although it should be recognised that such studies can be undertaken at a number of different scales and to different levels of intensity.

As an element of professional practice, assessment in its most general sense has been a key part of the administration of the Ancient Monuments legislation for over 100 years (Saunders 1983). It has also been a major element in the provision of archaeological advice through the planning system since the mid 1970s, when county archaeological officers began to be appointed and sites and monuments records (SMRs) established (Benson 1972; Burrow 1985).

Since the early 1980s, however, the number of assessment exercises of all kinds has increased dramatically as a result of rises in the number of planning applications, changes in the importance attached to archaeological resource management in the planning system, and the introduction to the UK of environmental assessment procedures. The general context of assessment procedures of all kinds within the planning system is conveniently summarised in PPG 16, *Archaeology and planning* which was issued in November 1990 after extensive consultations on draft versions (DoE 1990).

There is no doubt that over the last decade a great deal of assessment work has been carried out, much experience gained, and significant new archaeological data brought to light. Specific elements of assessment practices have been addressed through conference sessions, surveys, and guidance briefings: the process of field evaluation at the 1990 IFA Conference, environmental assessment procedures at the 1992 IFA conference (Ralston and Thomas 1993), the impact of PPG 16 (Pagoda Projects 1992), the yield of evaluation projects (Brereton and Lambrick 1990), and the assessment of road schemes (Lawson 1993). Despite all this little is known about the nature and scope of assessment practices as a whole, about the ways they have been executed, about their success, strengths, and weaknesses, or indeed about the general nature and extent of the archaeological data that have been collected. The assessments of assessments project was designed to discover and document these aspects of assessment, partly to provide a position statement, partly as a survey of what had been done, and partly as a critical review to stimulate the future positive development of the assessment process. The project was an assessment of the very business of assessment.

Aims and scope

The three main aims of the project were:

- to document the nature and extent of archaeological desk-based assessments, field evaluations, and environmental assessment programmes undertaken in England during the period 1982–91
- to prepare a list of completed assessment reports of various kinds, including wherever possible short summaries
- to review in general terms the approaches, sources, and methodologies deployed in a range of situations over the last ten years

Few limits were placed on the range of material to be considered, although a fundamental criterion for inclusion was that the assessment exercise should have been carried out in order to make a contribution to some kind of decision-making process in the general field of planning (eg determination of a planning application) or the administration of ancient monuments legislation (eg determination of an application for Scheduled Monument Consent). For this reason, exploratory archaeological work conducted for research or to assist in the positioning or costing of large-scale excavations has been excluded, as have all post-determination recording exercises such as watching briefs, recorded observations, and rescue excavations.

The project covered assessment work in all kinds of situation, both urban and rural, for all kinds of development (eg residential, commercial, industrial, infrastructure, and leisure), and at all scales (eg private, commercial or government-sponsored). Archaeological assessments which took the form of surveys connected with the formulation of estate management plans were, however, deliberately excluded.

The project focused on assessments carried out between the years 1982 and 1991, the cut-off date being 31st December 1991. It is recognised that this is an arbitrary end date for the study and that some projects which were undertaken within this period but which were not completed or reported upon until 1992 or later will have been omitted.

The results of the project are presented in two volumes. This report covers the descriptive and analytical aims of the work; a second catalogues the various assessment reports identified during the project (Darvill *et al* 1994). The second volume also includes short abstracts of the findings of the various studies.

Method statement

Introduction

Many individuals and organisations have been involved in assessments over the last decade, and with increasing organisational specialisation it is often the case that more than one organisation is involved in a single exercise. This specialisation is particularly noticeable in the case of the now widely recognised roles of curator and contractor/consultant. The former is typically involved in requesting, specifying, and ultimately using the results of an assessment, whereas the latter carries out the necessary searches, undertakes the fieldwork, and prepares a report. Such distinctions were not so clearly marked, if they were at all discernible, in the early years covered by the present study, but many archaeological organisations operating at the time of the survey had been in existence throughout the decade under scrutiny, even if their roles changed during this period.

Data were collected from July 1992 to June 1993. Three main avenues were used for data collection, archaeological curators, archaeological contractors/ consultants, and consolidated published and un-published records of various sorts. Each is discussed briefly below.

Archaeological curators

These are organisations with a defined or self-assumed remit to take care of the archaeological resource in the context of Ancient Monuments legislation, planning procedures, or estate management. They are most closely involved with the decision-making processes relating to the preservation and conservation of the archaeological resource, often as expert advisors. Appendix 1 lists the archaeological curators surveyed and shows the extent of their operational areas. They can be divided on organisational grounds into the following main groups:

- national bodies (eg English Heritage, National Trust)
- county archaeology sections (usually connected to county sites and monuments records)
- national Park archaeology sections
- district/borough/town archaeology sections

Contact was made with 97 archaeological curators, initially through a questionnaire circulated in May 1992. Responses were obtained from 71 (73%) of these in the form of self-completed questionnaires, relevant data returned by post, or through personal visits by members of the project team. The overall rate of return was high for a survey of this kind, possibly in part because of the extensive use of personal visits to assist in the collection of data. As a result overall coverage was good, although a few gaps exist where, because of local circumstances, it was not possible to respond by the close of the survey.

Archaeological contractors and consultants

These are organisations (in some cases an individual operating as a sole trader) who act on behalf of clients as advisors and/or undertake archaeological projects of various kinds on the same basis. The range of such projects is generally wide and varied, archaeological assessments of various kinds being only part of the portfolio of services offered. In some cases archaeological contractors and consultants operate independently, but in other cases they are part of multi-disciplinary practices. Traditionally, many curators based in local authorities have also acted as archaeological contractors through the provision of an integrated archaeological service (eg a county archaeological service). As the curatorial role of providing expert advice to planning authorities has increased the linkage between curatorial and contracting activities in a single body has been called into question on ethical grounds and concern has been widely expressed. It should be noted, however, that at the time of this survey a number of organisations operated an integrated service and that for much of the period documented in this study such arrangements were normal rather than exceptional.

In all, 71 contractors and consultants were included in the present survey. Appendix 2 lists those contacted and shows the location of their headquarters. It should be noted, however, that the operating territories of these contractors vary considerably, from a district- or city-based area to the whole of the country. Since no national consolidated register or list of archaeological contractors exists, and organisations come and go in the course of time, it is not possible to gauge precisely what percentage this represents of all the bodies that operated in England during the period covered by the survey. It is estimated, however, that it represents about 85% of all such organisations.

Published and unpublished records, databases, and libraries

Records of assessment programmes are available in a number of published and unpublished sources, although most relate to a specific geographical area or subject. Examples include the annual reviews or reports and periodic 'round-ups' of recent work published by, for example, the regional groups of the Council for British Archaeology, national and local archaeological societies, archaeological units and trusts, and county archaeology sections. These rarely provided the full range of data required for the study presented below, but were useful as checklists of what had been done and served as the starting point for locating reports. A few assessment exercises reported in these secondary sources have not been verified from other sources; this is indicated where relevant in the companion directory (Darvill *et al* 1994).

The main primary source referred to in this section is the collection of environmental statements held by the Institute of Environmental Assessment at its headquarters at East Kirkby in Lincolnshire. This important collection allows an overview of work that has taken place in the field of environmental assessment over the last few years and provides a central location at which reports can be consulted. Although the collection is not complete it is regarded as representative. The IEA has about 600 environmental statements undertaken in England to the end of 1991. Nothing comparable exists for specifically archaeological assessment reports.

Data collection

As already indicated, data from these various sources were assembled through a series of questionnaires and data entry forms. In some cases these were completed by the organisations to which they were sent, in other cases by members of the project team who visited the organisations surveyed and helped them to complete the questionnaires. All data gathered in this way were entered onto a series of databases (using Dbase IV), and these were interrogated to provide the quantifications presented later in this report. The databases also included bibliographic data and short abstracts which were used in the compilation of the companion volume (*ibid*).

The aim of the survey was to achieve blanket coverage rather than a statistically constituted sample, since one of the overall aims of the project was to assemble short summaries of work done. In order to attract widespread attention in the profession notice of the project and its aims was inserted in a number of archaeological periodicals, including *Conservation Bulletin* and *British Archaeological News*. Although it is recognised that some contractors and curators were not contacted it is estimated that coverage was generally good and that over 85% of reported assessment programmes have been identified. Specific constraints and limitations relating to data sources and data quality are discussed where relevant in later chapters.

The question of confidentiality was raised by a number of curators and contractors, and there was understandable reluctance to make available the findings of ongoing projects and those which had not yet formed the basis for a determination. This became less of a problem with the lapse of time after the cut-off date for the survey (ie after the end of 1991). Every effort has been made to respect the wishes of contractors and their clients with regard to confidentiality; in some cases projects may have been counted in the quantifications reported later in this volume but do not appear in the companion volume of abstracts. It may be noted in passing that any documents submitted to a local authority in support of a planning application are automatically in the public domain and available for consultation.

The quantifications presented in this volume are mainly raw counts or percentages based on such counts. Data are mainly grouped according to the year in which the work was undertaken or reported and the region in which it took place. Three broad geographical regions were defined using county boundaries current at the time of the survey. They correspond to the three operational regions used by the Conservation Division of English Heritage, North, Midlands, and South. Fig 1 shows the extent of each region. For some analyses the data for London are treated separately from the South region in which it lies. Changing arrangements for archaeology in London over the last two years have made it difficult to recover consistent and comprehensive coverage for the capital throughout the last decade.

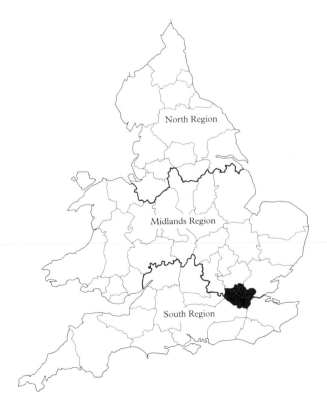

Fig 1 Regional divisions used in this study

Definitions and terminology

For the purposes of this study a number of recurrent sets of tasks have been categorised and labelled following common usage. It is recognised that these terms may not adequately describe work carried out in the early years covered by this survey, and some of the terms used here were not, and are not now, applied systematically or consistently. Where the present terminology has been used as a classification of reports or pieces of work every effort has been made to check the scope and nature of the work so that its contribution is accurately described. Terms like archaeological assessment and field evaluation were inconsistently applied in the material examined during this project, especially in the titles of reports. In classifying reports use has been made of content rather than title, with the result that studies called one thing by their originators may be classified as something else in this study. It may be hoped that in future terminology for different elements of the assessment process will be more consistently applied (*cf* ACAO 1993).

The following terms are used in this report to refer to different kinds of assessment. All have found general acceptance in the profession in recent years (*cf* Darvill and Gerrard 1992; ACAO 1993; English Heritage 1995):

Appraisal: the process of checking planning applications or development proposals to identify, using local knowledge and experience, those with a potential archaeological dimension which needs further clarification.

Detailed appraisal: a thorough review of the SMR and other sources to determine whether there may or may not be an archaeological dimension to a development proposal. This sometimes involves visually inspecting the site.

Desk-based assessment: primarily a desk-top exercise commissioned to consolidate, examine, and validate the recorded archaeological resource of an area potentially affected by development proposals. Usually involves visually inspecting the site but stops short of collecting and synthesising new data through fieldwork or other primary research. As outlined in PPG 16 (paragraph 20), where it is simply called 'archaeological assessment'.

Field evaluation: a systematic and problem-oriented programme of site investigation involving invasive and/or non-invasive fieldwork, designed to supplement and improve existing information to a level of confidence at which planning recommendations can be made, as outlined in PPG 16 (paragraph 21). It is assumed that an appraisal and/or desk-based assessment has taken place before field evaluation. The results of appraisals and/or archaeological assessments may be included in the report on field evaluation.

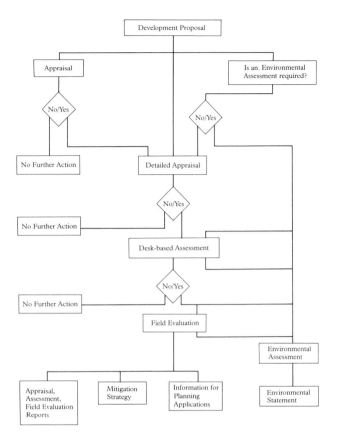

Fig 2 Main elements of assessment procedures

Environmental assessment: a multi-disciplinary programme of investigation which collects data from a defined archaeological resource and examines the likely effects of a proposed development programme on that resource. The results are called an environmental statement and its content and scope are defined by law.

These five task sets are related to each other and to a general process. Fig 2 shows in schematic form an idealised arrangement of procedures. At the time of the survey considerable regional variation still existed in the application of assessment procedures. The identification of assessment exercises relevant to each of these task sets can be based only on evidence of execution or outcome, typically a report or printed document of some kind.

The word 'assessment' is used in three ways through this report. First, in the general sense, as an estimate of the magnitude or quality of something (usually the archaeological resource). Secondly, as a general collective term to cover the process of gauging the nature, extent, and importance of the archaeological resource (ie covering all the procedures defined above). Thirdly, in the specific sense of a desk-based archaeological assessment or an environmental assessment as closely defined steps in the overall process of reviewing archaeological and environmental resources respectively. The term desk-based assessment or desk-based archaeological assessment is used here in the same way as the synonymous term 'archaeological assessment' is used in paragraph 20 of PPG 16 (DoE 1990).

The terms curator, contractor, and consultant have already been introduced to cover roles enacted by various kinds of archaeological organisation. These roles are not necessarily mutually exclusive.

Report structure and layout

This report is divided into seven chapters and broadly reflects the unfolding of the assessment process. In Chapter 2 attention is given to the development of the assessment process and some of the key principles which structure its use. Chapter 3 is concerned with appraisals and looks at the relationships between the changing levels of planning applications and the numbers of archaeologically significant proposals. Chapter 4 focuses on the commercial context of development by looking at the kinds of development and land use that are the subject of development proposals, and the ways in which assessment programmes are funded. Chapter 5 then examines in more detail the desk-based assessments and field evaluations carried out between 1982 and 1991, and Chapter 6 does the same for environmental assessment projects. Chapter 7 ends with some observations and conclusions. Two appendices provide details of the curators and contractors surveyed. No specific recommendations are made in this report; they have been included alongside the recommendations arising from the Southampton project in a separate publication issued by English Heritage (English Heritage 1995).

2 The idea of assessment

The development of assessment procedures and their place in decision-making

Assessments of the archaeological resource in the broadest sense are nothing new. The idea of carrying out some kind of survey to reveal the location and extent of archaeological remains before detailed investigation has a long history in the evolution of methodologies for excavating and researching archaeological sites. The way this sort of survey has developed and the contribution of the results to the decision-making process form an important part of the background to interpreting and understanding the results of this project as described in subsequent chapters.

The term 'trial trench' is commonly encountered in archaeological texts of the early twentieth century and refers to what might be regarded as the earliest systematic assessment method. The objective was usually to locate and target the best area for excavation within a known site or archaeologically rich landscape. Woolley (1930, 44) describes the process based on experience in the Near East. Here the practice was often to dig a long slit trench across a site and then to expand those areas which seemed most promising. The use of trial trenches did not find universal approval. Writing in the early 1950s, Mortimer Wheeler declared that 'The old practice of cutting trial trenches, of making sondages, as a preliminary to, or even in lieu of, area excavation was frequently a substitute for intelligent thinking and clear aiming. It was to a large extent 'shooting into the brown' on the off-chance of bringing down a bird. Trial trenches rarely prove anything, save of the most general kind.' (Wheeler 1954, 81)

After this condemnation he then goes on to identify one specific use, saying 'On the other hand, prejudice against trenching cannot be extended to sites where the preliminary problem is solely and simply to search for a superficially invisible structure ... The principle here advocated is that trenching should be employed, not as a normal method, but only when very special circumstances demand it.' (ibid, 82)

The kind of special circumstances referred to by Wheeler are of course regularly encountered, although more recent texts on field practice also emphasise the need, not only for trial trenches, but also for ground surveys of various types and for a thorough investigation of documentary records and previous work in the area (Webster 1963, 60).

The importance of what came to light through trial trenching was measured in terms of its academic potential and the likelihood of uncovering 'interesting' archaeology, which tended to be defined in terms of the spectacular rather than the prosaic. The concept of using careful reviews of existing knowledge, surveys, and/or trial trenching as a means of collecting information to help assess areas to be preserved rather than excavated or studied came later, although as Chapter 6 will show the methods used were carried over from research-oriented field practice.

The development of sites and monuments records as definitive and comprehensive statements of the archaeological resource in a defined area was a key factor in allowing archaeological interests to be represented in the town and country planning system. One of the primary concerns of the planning system is to balance the economic benefits of development with the conservation of the physical environment. This is achieved in two ways, through strategic planning and development control. Archaeological considerations have a place in both, although it is easy for archaeologists to overestimate their importance in the system as a whole.

Strategic planning provides the framework within which decisions on development control are taken. In addition to policies relating preservation to development, the archaeological content of a strategic plan might include policies which would allow a local authority to require applicants to provide adequate information about the archaeological aspects of proposed development, and, where necessary, to carry out desk-based assessments or field evaluations in order to provide that information.

Planning application procedures are at the heart of development control. Democratically elected committees take decisions on planning applications, usually with advice from professionally qualified officers and experts. It is incumbent on a planning committee, in addition to the full range of legally defined factors and constraints (eg Scheduled Monument legislation, strategic plans, and so on), to take account of 'any other relevant matters', and of any material considerations. Archaeology has always been a 'relevant matter', although under such a general heading little impact could be achieved without special lobbying. The definition of 'material considerations' is more interesting. Although there is considerable debate about what should be regarded as material considerations, they undoubtedly include matters specified as such in policy guidance from central government. DoE Planning Circular 8/87 specified for the first time that 'the desirability of preserving the [archaeological] monument and its setting is of course a material consideration' (paragraph 52). This position has been reiterated in PPG 16 (DoE 1990, paragraph 27), and together with the policies in strategic plans represents the basis on which archaeology is included in the decision-making process within the planning system.

The need for information which will assist planning committees in their work and allow planning officers to form sustainable views to report to their committees may seem obvious, but it has taken many years to put in place the mechanisms for obtaining this information. In addition to invoking strategic plan policies and the advice contained in PPG 16, local planning authorities have statutory powers to request background information in advance of planning applications through the *Town and Country Planning (Applications Regulations) 1988* (SI 1812). The need for information to be made available to those who will make the decisions is fundamental to the successful operation of assessment procedures throughout the planning process. PPG 16 is ambiguous on this point: paragraph 21 suggests that archaeological field evaluations should be arranged and carried out 'before any decision on the planning application is taken', but paragraph 22 suggests that local planning authorities can expect developers to provide the results of desk-based archaeological assessments and field evaluations 'as part of their application'. The difference in timing is significant; the latter sequence of events is the ideal, but the former represents the pragmatic solution adopted by many developers. Carrying out the field evaluation between the time an application is first lodged with a local authority and its determination also has the advantage of allowing time for the identification of other, non-archaeological, factors which may cause an application to fail. This certainly seems to save time and expense, but is also a positive contribution to conservation since field evaluation itself can be destructive of the resource. The need to have the right information available at the right time was central to Darvill and Gerrard's formulation of a five-staged approach to the integration of archaeological resource management within the development process (Darvill and Gerrard 1992), a model since adopted by English Heritage and ACAO (ACAO 1993, 4). The five stages consist of appraisal, archaeological assessment, field evaluation, strategy formulation, and strategy implementation, the first three constituting the general process of assessment discussed in this report.

Assessment practices have evolved in two other main areas, among statutory undertakers and government departments, and in the context of environmental assessment procedures.

In the case of the statutory undertakers and government departments (for example British Gas, Thames Water, and the Department of Transport) assessment procedures have been developed which broadly mirror those applied elsewhere. The timescale for the planning, researching, and execution of developments in these sectors is often rather longer-term than in other sectors of the development industry and in some cases the sequence of consultations and public inquiries is prescribed by legislation. The special nature of some of the developments carried out in these sectors, especially the linear nature and unusual engineering requirements of road and pipeline construction, means that the basic model of assessment procedures must be varied (Lawson 1993).

Assessment procedures in the sphere of environmental assessment, including timetabling and consultation, are partly prescribed in the legislation which requires such assessments, the *Town and Country Planning (Assessment of Environmental Effects) Regulations 1988* (SI 1199).

Professional judgement

All archaeological assessments are both based upon, and serve to inform, professional judgments. Here it is important to distinguish between professional judgements based on current best practice and accepted procedures and personal opinions which reflect only what the person offering the opinion thinks. The place of such judgements in archaeology has recently been reviewed by Startin (1993) with particular reference to the assessment of monuments for the Monuments Protection Programme, but the same principles apply to the assessment process. As an exercise, assessment procedures develop from intuitive judgements (ie appraisal) through what may be described as peer-aided judgements (ie desk-based archaeological assessments) towards well-structured assessments which may be classed as controlled trials or scientific experiments (ie field evaluations). As these tasks become more structured, the level of analysis, the costs, and the likelihood of achieving a reliable outcome also increase.

Professional judgements of the sort used in assessment procedures are neither right nor wrong, because there are no absolutes involved, only the interpretation through experience and expertise of indicators relating to defined states of the resource. As Table 1 shows, there are four possible outcomes of a judgement relating to the presence or absence of archaeological deposits in a given assessment area, the archaeological deposits may be existent or non-existent and the identification procedure (diagnosis of the indicators) may be correct or incorrect. The optimum positions in the matrix are those indicating a correct diagnosis, but it must be accepted that this can never be achieved for 100% of cases; a success rate of 80% would probably indicate a highly commendable performance.

The survey revealed that many archaeologists believe that successful assessment programmes are those which reveal archaeology. As the above remarks indicate, this

Table 1 Matrix summarising the possible outcomes of an assessment exercise

	correct diagnosis	*incorrect diagnosis*
archaeological deposits present	true positive (present)	false negative (absent)
archaeological deposits absent	true negative (absent)	false positive (present)

cannot logically be so. A successful project is one in which a correct diagnosis is made. A comparison with the case of a potentially sick person visiting a doctor is apt: the success of the visit depends on the doctor correctly diagnosing the complaint and prescribing appropriate treatment, not on the severity of the condition itself. The metaphor is perhaps even more apposite if the process of diagnosis is considered. Simple common complaints can usually be recognised quickly and easily with a high degree of success, but there are more intractable cases where elaborate tests and analyses are needed before a diagnosis is reached. Even in the life and death reality of the medical profession, diagnoses are not always correct.

Understanding the conceptual basis of assessment and the real object of undertaking the process is crucial to the analysis of methodologies and the expectations of those involved in the work.

The concept of importance

Knowing whether or not there are archaeological deposits within a study area is not in itself enough to satisfy the overall objectives of most assessments. All archaeological remains are important for one reason or another (at least to archaeologists), but some are more important than others. The concept of variable importance underpins accepted approaches to archaeological resource management. The socially defined value set which lies behind the definition of what can be regarded as important is outside the scope of this report (see Darvill 1993 and Startin 1993 for discussions with additional references).

The Secretary of State for the Environment issued criteria in 1983 (DoE 1983) to assist in judging whether or not a given ancient monument qualified for scheduling on the grounds of 'national importance'. The criteria, which have been widely promulgated since, were period, rarity, documentation, group value, survival/ condition, fragility/vulnerability, diversity, and potential. Since 1983 the criteria have been systematically reviewed and developed for individual situations, most notably the Monuments Protection Programme (Darvill *et al* 1987). The extent to which the concept of importance is applied in the assessment process is discussed at length in later chapters.

3 Appraisals in England 1982–91

Introduction

Appraisal is the stage common to all assessment programmes but it is probably the most important but the least well-documented of the stages. The question posed is simply 'Is there an archaeological dimension to this proposal or application which needs to be examined?' In some cases an answer can be quickly and easily given, for example 'no' in the case of a planning application for a new warden's hut in a nature reserve on a reinstated gravel pit. Others might be more difficult to answer and involve recourse to existing records and perhaps even a site visit.

For convenience, appraisals are divided into two groups: simple appraisals of the kind which can be done from local knowledge and experience, and detailed appraisals involving searches and checks. In only a few cases will appraisals give rise to formal reports. The outcomes of many will be given verbally, as notes on case files, in correspondence or in the case of negative outcomes as no action at all.

The starting point for a consideration of appraisals is an understanding of the pattern of planning applications processed by local authorities over the last decade. All the curators surveyed were asked for data about the number of applications processed and most were able to supply relevant data, except in northern counties for which data are available only from 1988 onwards.

Fig 3 shows an analysis of total planning applications by region for the years 1982–91. The figures are based on returns from archaeological curators around the country, missing data from some counties or years being calculated through the use of regional averages. The data missing from the counties of the south of England may have led to the regional average created for this area being only a conservative estimate of the true level of planning applications and development.

Overall, the number of applications recorded during the survey is slightly less than official statistics for the same periods; the number of applications submitted in 1991, for example, was 512,000 (information from Government Statistical Service). The lower figures reported by archaeologists probably reflect fallout rates, linked applications, and the exclusion of those which never reached their attention. The total number of applications is consistently greatest in the Midland region, although this is partly accounted for by the shape and size of the three regional units as defined for this study. It is important to note that at a general level all three areas show similar profiles, with a gradual year-on-year increase through the 1980s followed by a decline after the turn of the decade. The detail is more revealing. In the South the peak occurs in 1988, in the Midlands a year later in 1989, and in the North another year later in 1990. The graphs also suggest that the fall-off after the peak is greatest in the North, slightly less in the Midlands and least marked in London and the South.

In the South region the decline in the number of planning applications occurs at a rate of 8,000 per year after 1988, the peak showing a regional total for that year of 140,000 following a steady average rise of 12,000 a year through the 1980s. This trend is paralleled in London. In the Midlands, the peak in 1989 was approximately 190,000 applications after a steady rise averaging 15,000 a year since 1986. Since 1989 planning applications for the region have declined by around 20,000 in each of the following two years to the 1991 level of 150,000 applications. In the North region the years 1988 to 1990 show an annual increase of around 30,000 to peak at 180,000 followed by a decrease to 120,000 in 1991.

All these trends reflect general economic conditions of growth followed by recession. For archaeological resource management, the implications of these trends are twofold. First, although there has been a significant diminution in the absolute number of applications over the last two or three years the overall level of applications remains high and is typically 50–70% higher in this recession than in the early 1980s. Second, long-term planning can no longer assume linear growth of workloads and annual increases in the number of applications, as might have been predicted in the early 1990s. Future trends might be more realistically modelled in terms of a cyclical pattern of growth and retraction.

Appraisal rates

No data are available about the level of appraisal that takes place, as this relies mainly on local knowledge and a periodic (often weekly) scanning of circulated lists of planning applications prepared by local authorities.

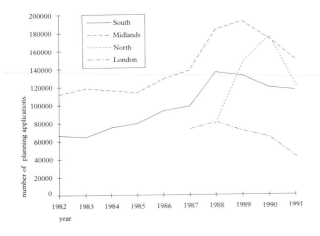

Fig 3 Estimated total planning applications 1982–91

Observations made during the survey suggest that throughout England there is an acceptable coverage of such appraisals but that some districts are neither consistently nor systematically covered. Information about the level of this kind of work is sparse because the results of appraisal are almost never recorded. The Pagoda report (Pagoda Projects 1992) notes that nearly all planning applications are appraised at some level.

Detailed appraisals are better documented. Fig 4 shows in diagrammatic form the changing pattern of detailed appraisals through the three regions by year. Again no data are available from the northern counties until 1988. In absolute terms, the number of detailed appraisals undertaken in the Midlands is consistently higher than for either of the other two areas. The profile for the Midlands is also rather different from that of either the South or the North, with a peak in 1984 and a near-continuous rise in numbers subsequently. In the South there was a fall in growth in 1985 leading to a peak in appraisal numbers in 1989, the same year as the peak in the North.

The proportion of detailed appraisals to the number of planning applications is shown by region on Figs 5a, b, and c. The variations in the percentage of applications appraised clearly indicate a variation in approach to the question of archaeological resource management. The rate of detailed appraisal appears to have been highest in the Midlands during the period of this review, exceeding figures in the South by about 2% a year with a maximum difference of 3.75% in 1991 (a small percentage, but a large number considering the overall level of applications involved). The figures for the North are more closely related to those of the Midlands, but once again a significant difference (3%) is notable in 1991. These variations are not related to the total number of planning applications. Had this been the case it might have been expected that the Midlands, with its high level of planning applications, would have been able to record only a low percentage of

detailed appraisals. This apparent lack of correlation is surprising given that there are unlikely to be marked regional variations in the pattern of development to explain it. The implication is that during the period covered by this review there was no consistent procedure for the selection of planning applications for detailed appraisal. At an inter-regional level the

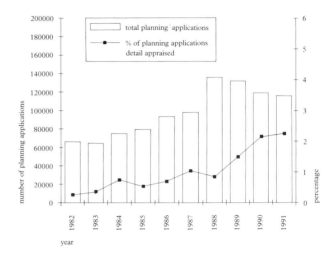

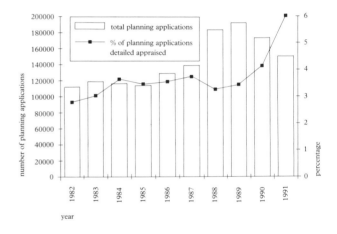

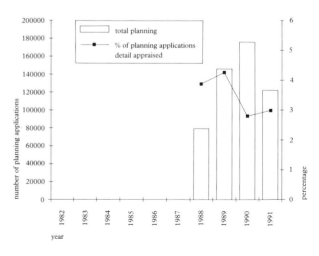

Fig 5 Estimated number of planning applications and the percentage appraised in detail, (top) South region, (middle) Midlands region, and (bottom) North region

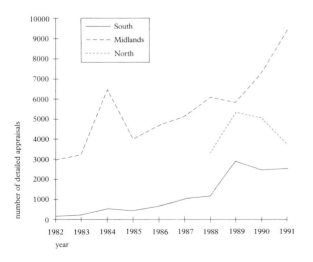

Fig 4 Recorded number of detailed appraisals carried out between 1982–91

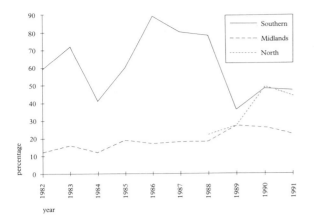

Fig 6 Detailed appraisals producing an archaeological dimension

variations in the number of detailed appraisals may well reflect differences in the availability of curatorial staff to carry out such work, particularly in recent years when the quantity of detailed appraisals carried out has risen so considerably.

Appraisal outcomes

The percentage of detailed appraisals initiated by curators which produced a positive outcome, confirming that there was an archaeological dimension to the proposals, varied considerably between regions (Fig 6). In the South, performance over time has been cyclical, with reductions in 1984 and 1989, and since 1989 a fairly consistent return at about 45% is evident, although in London this has been lower (Fig 7). Taking into account the relatively low number of detailed appraisals undertaken, the inverse relationship since 1986 between the number of such appraisals carried out, and the rate of positive outcome with archaeology present (*cf* Fig 4), it may be suggested that traditionally the selection of applications for appraisal was closely targeted, with a higher expectation of confirming the presence of archaeological deposits than of simply establishing presence/absence. This position has,

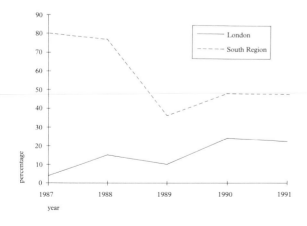

Fig 7 Detailed appraisals producing an archaeological dimension in London (excluding the City) and the South region

however, shifted to one in which appraisals are undertaken more routinely with an open-minded brief to check for archaeology rather than to confirm suspicions. Two possible contributory factors may explain this pattern. The completion of a sites and monuments record system for all counties in England has led to the establishment of screening systems to review planning applications, and PPG 16 proposed that prospective developers should make early contact with the relevant archaeological curator. Pagoda Projects (1992, 6) reports that such consultation has increased, although mainly on the part of large developers.

In the Midlands region the percentage of detailed appraisals which have produced an archaeological dimension has remained remarkably stable at between 10% and 20% through the period of study, with a maximum level in 1989. The North region increased steadily to peak at about the same level as the South region in 1990, since when both have declined slightly.

Taking all this together, there was a clear upward trend over the period covered by the study in the number of planning applications which, following detailed appraisal, had a positive outcome in the sense of identifying an archaeological dimension which had to be addressed. In the Midlands region this trend appears to be continuing, although its future projection in the South and the North regions is less clear. Across the country some 15,635 detailed appraisals (*c* 4% of all planning applications) were undertaken in 1991, an average of 301 per week across the country.

Who does appraisals?

At the time of the survey there were 77 curatorial officers in English county councils (including county archaeological officers, assistant county archaeological officers, etc), 14 city archaeologists, 9 borough district/community archaeologists, 5 National Park archaeological officers with curatorial duties, and 4 Development Corporations with conservation officers who had some curatorial responsibility for archaeology. In theory, some parts of the country were within the domain of more than one curator because of the multi-tiered local government system. In practice, however, it was found that local arrangements existed to distribute responsibility. This implies that it is sometimes difficult to determine which organisation hosts the relevant curator.

Arrangements for carrying out appraisals at both general and detailed levels vary. In the majority of English counties (93%), the main identified curator is within the county authority, usually the county archaeological officer, an assistant, or the sites and monuments record officer. Where these officers are within the planning department of the authority the usual method of screening applications is by immediate response to the lists of applications circulated within the department. These lists comprise all the applications made directly to the county (eg minerals, waste, etc) and the district or borough lists of local applications that are passed on to the county authority. Where the county curators are outside a planning department there is typically less direct contact with lists of planning applications. For instance, some curators working in museums, libraries, leisure, or resources departments receive planning application lists which have already been screened within the planning department, which passes on for appraisal only those considered to be of possible heritage or archaeological potential. The basis on which such screening is done is not known.

Where a local authority such as a city, district, or borough has its own curatorial office or an arrangement with an outside conservation or archaeological organisation, the county curator is often unaware of or not consulted upon local applications relating to these areas. At the time of the survey only 48% of the county authorities were found to be the sole archaeological curators within their counties.

Numerically, the majority of appraisals are carried out by archaeological curators either as a result of inquiries directed to them from developers or as the first response to formal planning applications. However, the increase in pre-planning stage interest in archaeological matters encouraged by PPG 16 (paragraph 19) may precipitate greater numbers of independently-commissioned appraisal-type reviews. The survey recorded the existence of a small number (<50) of such privately commissioned appraisals in 1991, but did not systematically survey consultants and contractors to quantify this kind of work. A number of contractors mentioned that appraisal-type inquiries were on the increase. Some planning consultancies are known to carry out detailed appraisals on behalf of clients for all or most of the projects they handle, as a routine way of familiarising themselves with the project and assembling background information. It is easy to envisage that such reports may become one of the standard 'searches' instigated by solicitors or developers before entering into agreements on the acquisition of land.

4 The commercial context

The kinds of development covered

The range of development types subject to desk-based archaeological assessment or field evaluation is intimately related to the scope of planning legislation and to economic and social trends which influence developers in bringing forward particular kinds of proposals at different times. Thus, for example, the rise in the number of desk-based assessments and field evaluations relating to golf course proposals is a result of the rise in popularity of this sport through the late 1980s, whereas in contrast the decline in proposed office-block development in the early 1990s is a reflection of over-provision in a time of economic recession. In the same way, ongoing land uses or land-use changes which are not covered by the definition of development in the planning legislation or which do not require permissions of any sort will not usually be covered by desk-based assessment or field evaluation exercises. This exclusion relates to many agricultural activities.

Fig 8 shows an analysis of the main kinds of development which have been the subject of desk-based archaeological assessments in recent years. Two points are especially noteworthy: firstly, the early concentration on such fundamental development type as roadlines, minerals, and housing, and secondly, the greater diversity of development types subject to desk-based assessment in 1990 and 1991. This suggests that PPG 16 had an impact in extending these desk-based studies to all kinds of development. In 1991 the development types subject to desk-based assessments were, in order of importance, road schemes (20%), golf courses (12%) pipelines (11%), urban commercial developments (9%), and mineral extraction (8%).

A similar set of trends is visible among field evaluations. Fig 9 provides an analysis of major development types by region. The wide spread of work carried out in 1991 is especially clear, the overall breakdown of work between types of development site being urban commercial developments (16%), urban residential developments (12%), road schemes (9%), mineral extraction sites (8%), and leisure facilities (5%). Regional variations can be seen, however, for example with differences in the level of field evaluations for mineral extraction focusing in the South throughout the decade, whereas in recent years the numbers of field evaluations for housing schemes in the North have exceeded those for similar developments in the South.

Turning to minor development types, Fig 10 shows the wide spread (not subdivided for region). The rise in

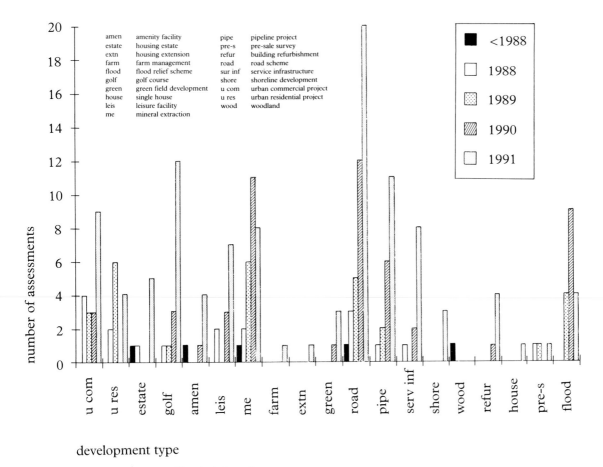

Fig 8 Development types covered by desk-based assessments

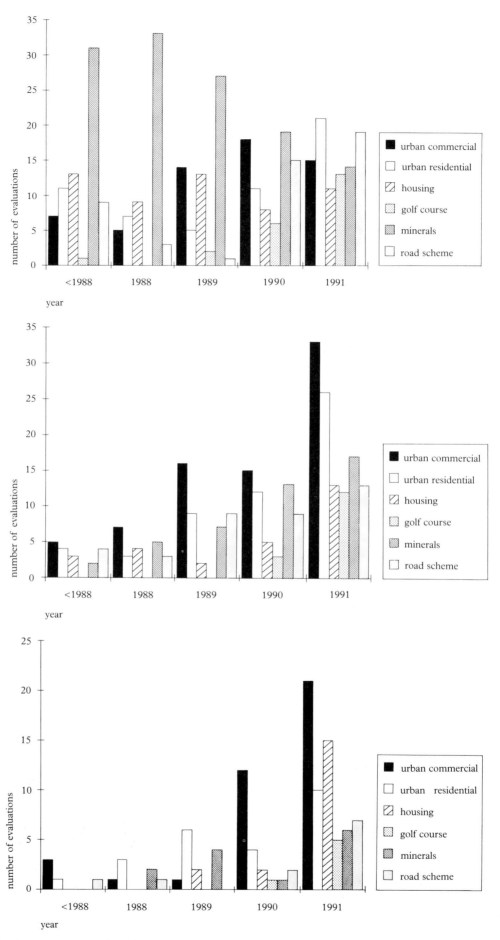

Fig 9 Major development types evaluated by year, (top) South region, (middle) Midlands region, and (bottom) North region

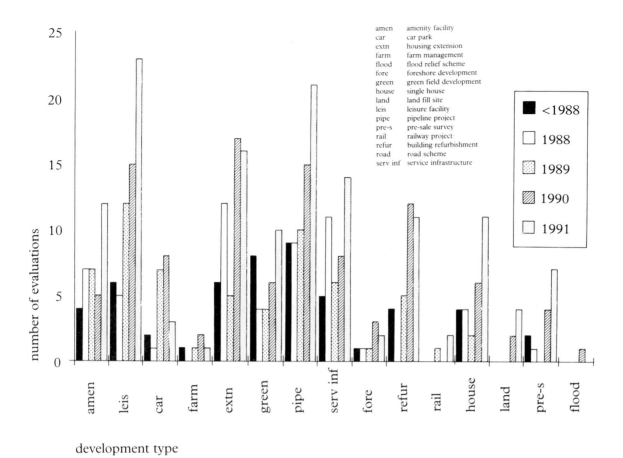

amen   amenity facility
car   car park
extn   housing extension
farm   farm management
flood   flood relief scheme
fore   foreshore development
green   green field development
house   single house
land   land fill site
leis   leisure facility
pipe   pipeline project
pre-s   pre-sale survey
rail   railway project
refur   building refurbishment
road   road scheme
serv inf   service infrastructure

Fig 10 Minor development types evaluated by year

field evaluations related to leisure facilities, pipelines, building refurbishment, and landfills is particularly notable.

The size of development areas subject to desk-based archaeological assessment and field evaluation is also relevant in this context and is analysed by region in Fig 11. In the case of desk-based assessments only a small sample of cases is available, 79. It seems that the study areas for desk-based assessments fall towards the larger end of the spectrum. This is especially noticeable for the North, where the small sample available suggests that only large site areas are subject to desk-based assessment. In the case of field evaluations, all three regions show a similar pattern throughout the course of the last decade, with a shift from an emphasis on the field evaluation of small areas (generally less than 1ha) to a situation in 1991 in which larger areas (over 20ha) made up the largest percentage of field evaluation exercises in the South and Midlands and the second largest percentage in the North.

Land-use in the development area

Land use is a significant factor in the preservation of archaeological remains (Darvill 1987) and is also relevant to the choice of methods for the assessment of the archaeological resource and for the development of mitigation strategies. Because desk-based assessments

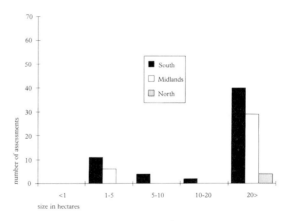

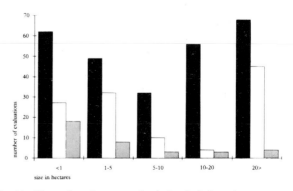

Fig 11 Sizes of study areas, (top) for desk-based assessments and (bottom) for field evaluations

and field evaluations are being undertaken on an increasingly large scale, there is often more than one land use type within the study area. Of those desk-based archaeological assessments covering an area greater than 5ha, over 50% covered more than one land-use type.

Thirteen land-use types were defined, based on those described elsewhere with reference to archaeological resource management (ibid), but with the addition of industrial land, derelict land, and foreshore. Fig 12 shows the annual distribution of desk-based assessments by land-use type since 1988. Overall, the most common land-use type for desk-based assessment is arable (50%), followed by pasture (36%), built-up land (28%), woodland (18%), and parkland (12%). These proportions are greater by up to 10% than would be expected from the percentage of England which each covers (MAFF 1982). This disparity is in part a reflection of the geographical situations favoured for development, but it also provides an illustration of the selection of areas and development types appropriate for desk-based assessment. For this reason, large-scale projects in previously undeveloped rural settings and small-scale projects in urban areas where documentation is good dominate the picture. Diachronic trends are also evident, most notably the relative decrease in the percentage of desk-based archaeological assessments in arable land as the number of projects in minor land-use types such as the uplands and heathlands increased.

The land-use types covered by field evaluation projects follow broadly the same pattern as for desk-based assessments (Fig 13), although there is more emphasis on derelict land. These variations can be seen as factors of the different situations in which desk-based assessments and field evaluations were used.

Figs 12 and 13 demonstrate the diversification in land-use types which have been subject to desk-based assessment and field evaluation in 1990, especially in coastal and riverside areas, wetland, heathland, and on upland moors. Since there is no reason to believe that this reflects an increase in development in these areas it must be assumed that it is a product of the increased recognition by archaeologists of the archaeological value and potential of these landscapes.

The funding of desk-based assessments and field evaluations

Throughout the period of this study the number and percentage of desk-based assessment and field evaluations funded by commercial sector developers have increased, but other trends are also present. Figs 14 and 15 show analyses of patterns of funding in desk-based assessments and field evaluations respectively. In the case of desk-based assessments the most notable trend is the diversification of funding. In the early years covered by the study, when relatively few desk-based assessments were carried out (cf Fig 14 with Fig 17),

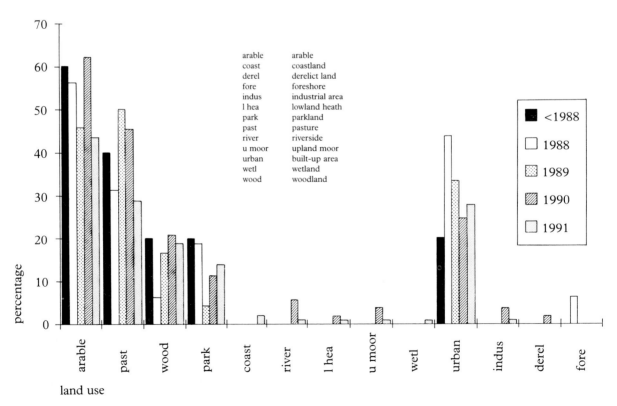

arable — arable
coast — coastland
derel — derelict land
fore — foreshore
indus — industrial area
l hea — lowland heath
park — parkland
past — pasture
river — riverside
u moor — upland moor
urban — built-up area
wetl — wetland
wood — woodland

Fig 12 Land-use types recorded within desk-based assessment study areas (including multiple land-uses). Shown as a percentage of the total number of desk-based assessments recorded; sample size 190

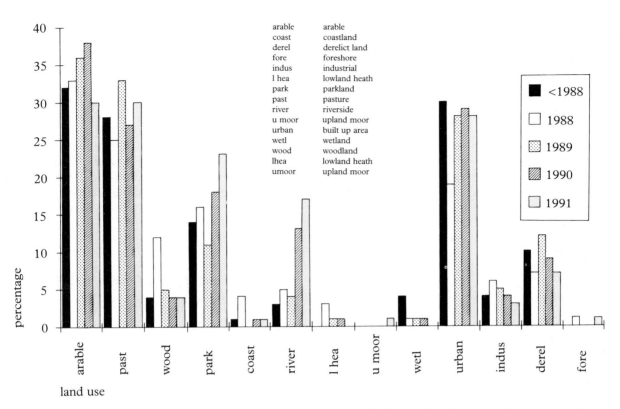

Fig 13 Land-use types recorded within field evaluation study areas (including multiple land-uses for projects). Shown as a percentage of the total number of field evaluations recorded; sample size 957

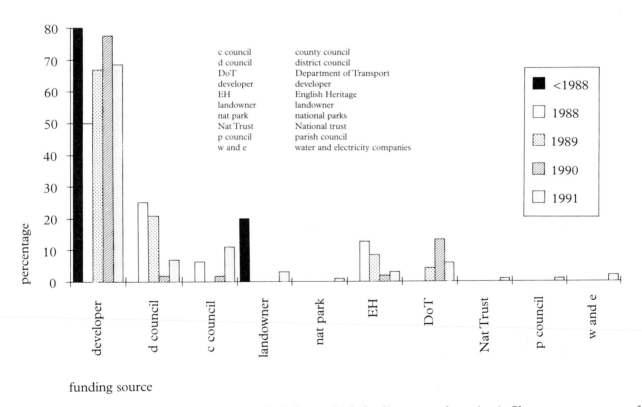

Fig 14 Funding sources for desk-based assessments (including multiple funding sources for projects). Shown as a percentage of the total number of desk-based assessments each year; sample size 199

developers in the private sector funded all such work, but since 1988 many other organisations have become involved, often in their capacity as facilitators of development. For field evaluation there is also evidence to suggest that the increase in developer funding is levelling off, with the proportion of privately funded projects decreasing in 1990 by *c* 3%. However, the introduction of PPG 16 provided fresh impetus to the

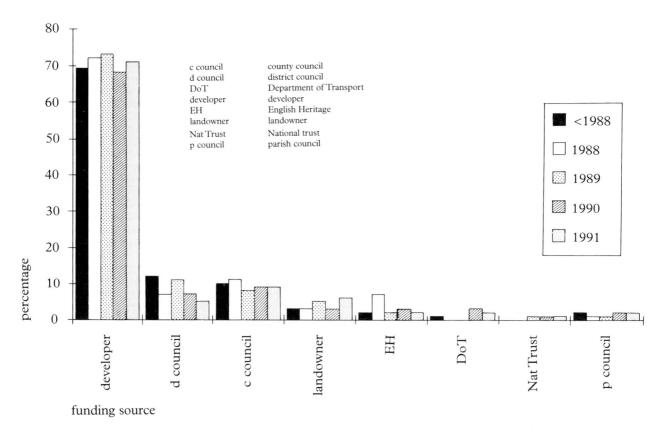

Fig 15 Funding sources for field evaluations (including multiple funding sources for projects). Shown as a percentage of the total number of field evaluations each year; sample size 1045

trend towards commercial sector funding, and in 1991 funding from this source accounted for some 70% of all funding for field evaluations. A recent survey by RESCUE revealed that developer funding of archaeology amounted to £15.5 million in 1990–91 (Spoerry 1992, 32).

The remaining projects were undertaken by bodies in the public sector. As has been noted, the proportion of publicly funded desk-based assessments rose in 1991, as did the variety of bodies undertaking assessment work (a diversification presumably to be seen also in the private sector). The range of bodies funding field evaluation does not show the same diversification through time, probably because field evaluation is a longer-established technique. Another point of note is the decrease in the proportion of funding for desk-based archaeological assessments in 1990 by such bodies as District Councils and English Heritage. One reason for this decline in English Heritage funding is the fact that the Department of Transport has, since 1989, increasingly assumed responsibility for desk-based assessments of national road building programmes (Wainwright 1992). In recent years this has also been extended to field evaluation programmes (Fig 15).

5 Desk-based assessments and field evaluations 1982–91

Desk-based assessment

How many, where, and when?

The number of desk-based assessments undertaken in all areas has increased considerably from one or two per year before 1988 to 97 cases in 1991. In total, 199 desk-based archaeological assessments were recorded during the survey, and in addition a large number of field evaluations incorporated a degree of desk-based study (see this chapter, Background data). Fig 16 (page 20) shows the regional variations in the distribution of desk-based assessments through time, Fig 17 shows the overall trend and regional variations as a histogram. The gradual expansion across the country of desk-based archaeological assessment procedures from a primary core area in central Southern England is very clearly shown on Fig 16. Alongside the geographical spread of desk-based assessment procedures there is an increase in the number of desk-based assessments in each area. The steady rise is clearest in the South region, the Midlands peaked in 1990, with smaller numbers in 1991, and the trend in the North region was slightly erratic until 1991 when a rise of equal proportions to that in the South can be seen. The upward trend in the use of desk-based assessments even without the impact of PPG 16 reflected in the 1991

figure is clear, and presumably reflects the value placed upon a phased response to the identification of archaeological problems by first drawing upon known sources. It may also reflect greater confidence among curators in the assessment process itself.

In total, some 50% of all desk-based assessments to date have been in the Southern counties, Midland and Northern counties accounting for 35% and 15% each (Fig18). Desk-based archaeological assessment is now widely practised in England, although the number of such exercises undertaken remains relatively small, and in 1991 averaged two a week across the country.

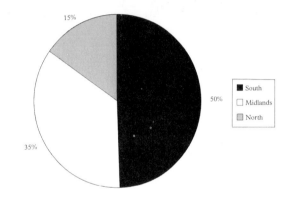

Fig 18 Desk-based assessments for 1982–91 by region; sample size 202

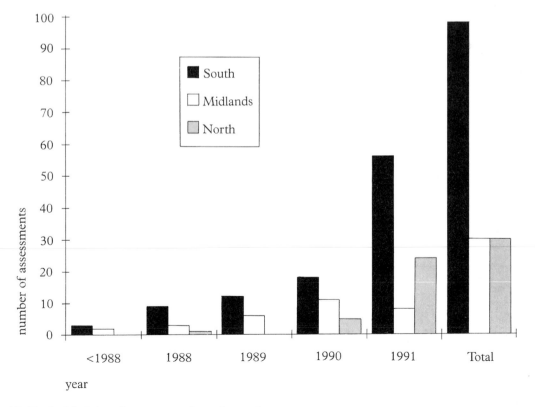

Fig 17 Total of desk-based assessments by region and year

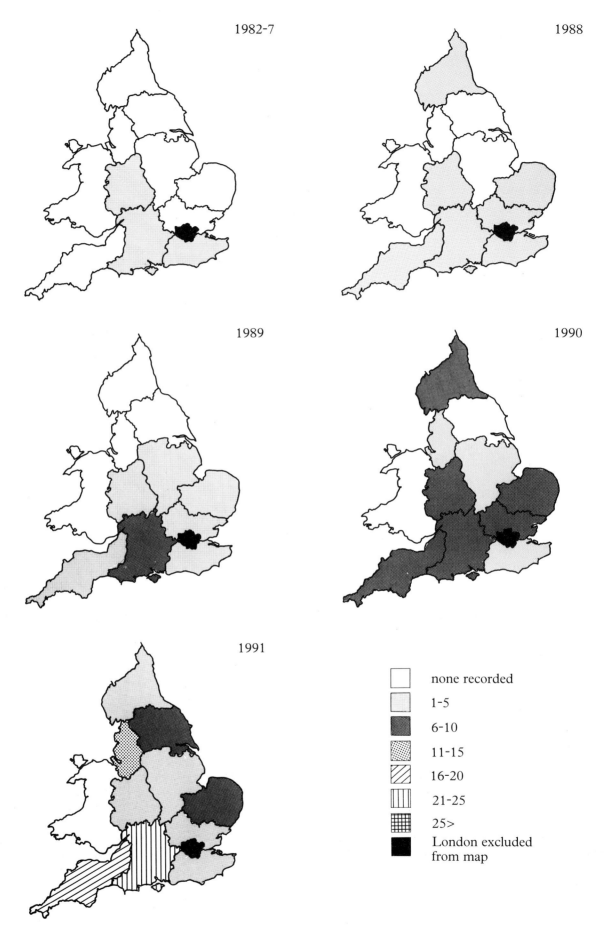

Fig 16 Geographical distribution of desk-based assessment by year

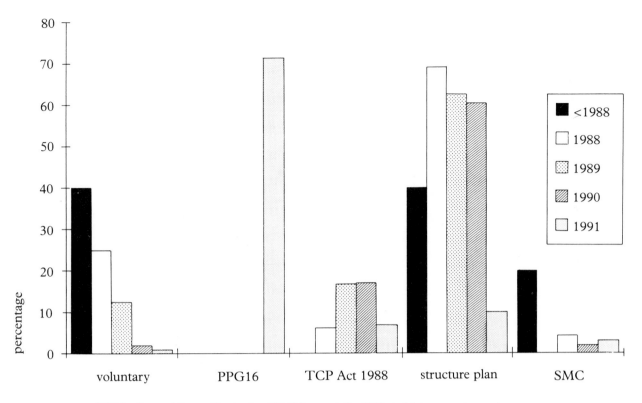

prompt (TCP Act Town and Country Planning Acts 1988-90 (as amended);   SMC scheduled monument consent)

Fig 19 Prompts for desk-based assessments by year

The basis of selection and brief setting

PPG 16 encourages prospective developers to commission their own desk-based assessments by a professionally qualified archaeological organisation or consultant (DoE 1990, paragraph 20). The need for an assessment must logically follow on from some kind of appraisal. A very small proportion of the desk-based assessments examined in this study, four from 1990 and seven from 1991, were found to have followed on directly from a detailed appraisal, the remaining 95% presumably resulting from an informal appraisal of some kind. This suggests that the majority of desk-based assessments represent the first documented stage of assessment for prospective developments.

Two main factors can be seen to influence the decision to use a desk-based assessment: the size of the development and the context of the work, either urban or rural. The majority of desk-based assessments are carried out for large-scale developments, and the desk-based assessment often serves as a rapid-scan technique for the identification of areas of archaeological potential which would be too large for detailed field evaluation to be applied consistently or economically. A disproportionate number of desk-based assessments on small-scale developments occur in an urban context, where there is more documentary material and the available detail allows closer analysis of individual sites.

The existence of Scheduled Monuments on a potential development site might be expected to influence the need for a desk-based assessment, but this does not seem to be the case. The study examined the incidence of Scheduled Monuments within the areas covered by desk-based archaeological assessment programmes. In 1988 some 33% of the desk-based assessments included Scheduled Monuments, but by 1991 this had fallen to 16.5%. This may reflect the avoidance by developers of sites known to contain obstacles to their planning applications, but more probably reflects the increasing confidence of curators in asking for desk-based assessments whether or not Scheduled Monuments are involved.

Prevailing guidance (ie PPG 16) and best professional practice are factors in prompting the use of a desk-based assessment. Fig 19 shows an analysis of the prompts which brought about the desk-based archaeological assessment projects identified in this study. It is clear that before 1988 voluntary production was a significant contributor, but that since then the proportion of voluntary assessment has declined.

When desk-based assessments are commissioned some form of brief or specification is required. Fig 20 shows an analysis of the sources of brief for the desk-based assessments in this study. It is interesting to note that the client and the local planning authorities make very minor contributions to the picture. Contractors were the main sources of briefs (ie design and execute contracts) before 1988, but since then county

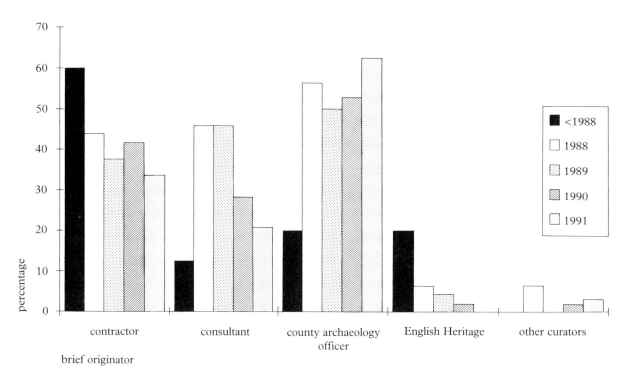

Fig 20 Authors of desk-based assessment briefs as a percentage of the total recorded desk-based assessments; sample size 199

archaeological officers and more recently archaeological consultants have become involved in setting briefs, although contractors have maintained a fairly steady participation at between 30% and 40%. In 1990 and 1991 the role of consultants in setting briefs declined in proportion to the rise in contributions by county archaeological officers. The emerging role of the curator at the hub of the assessment process is very clear from the trends visible in the setting of briefs. Some model briefs have already been published (English Heritage 1992a and 1992b; ACAO 1993). See also the draft standards published by the IFA (1993a and b).

Who does the work?

Contractors and consultants carry out most desk-based archaeological assessments, although some are prepared by curators. In organisational terms it is interesting to note that in addition to the usual range of units and trusts a number of university departments are involved in the preparation of desk-based assessments.

The first businesses to produce desk-based archaeological assessments as reports separate from the fieldwork stage of the study were in the South (in 1984). The Midlands first began to produce this sort of report in 1986 and the North in 1988. The total number of businesses involved in assessment work each year has shown a steady rise since 1987, with a slight fluctuation between 1988 and 1989. After 1989 the rise was very rapid, and the survey recorded a total of 35 firms undertaking desk-based assessments (48% of those carrying out field evaluations). Fig 21 shows the

number of new businesses (ie those recorded for the first time) entering into the production of desk-based assessments for the period 1984–91. The geographical location of new businesses entering into archaeological assessment work each year does not accurately reflect the regional patterns in the production of desk-based archaeological assessments. The South shows the closest correlation, with the rise in the number of desk-based assessments through time broadly matching the rise in the number of new businesses. For the rest of the country no direct correlation can be made, presumably because of the increase in size of existing firms, the lack of territoriality in firms undertaking desk-based assessments, and the state of business confidence. At a national level, however, it is interesting to note that the number of businesses entering into assessment work in 1990 and 1991 for the first time (13 and 17 respectively) was at its highest, despite the downturn in the economy and the pace of development at this time. This was identified in the Pagoda Report as being a result of the impact of PPG 16 (Pagoda Projects 1992). New consultancies are a major element of this increase in the level of business; it may be noted that such organisations do not usually require as much initial capitalisation or manpower resources as those undertaking fieldwork.

Sources of data used

Two main methods are employed for desk-based assessments, searches through existing sources and field checking. All the desk-based assessments in the study used searches of existing sources, but only 65% of projects used visual inspection.

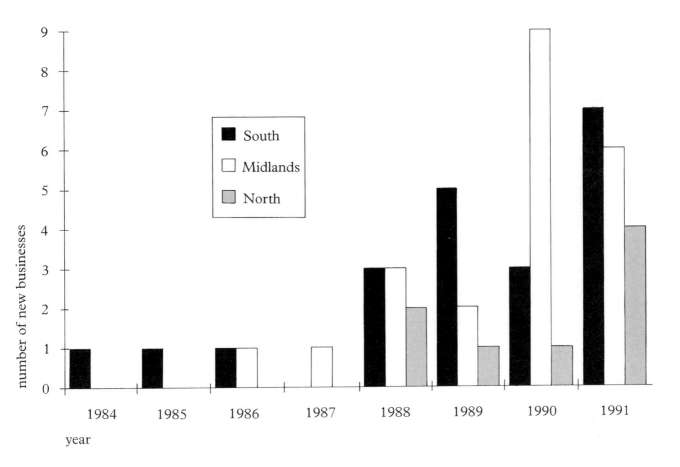

Fig 21 New business entering into desk-based assessment work each year

The sources usually consulted during assessment work can be seen as having three main roles, the identification of sites and monuments, the definition of the extent of archaeological deposits, and the provisional determination of archaeological importance. Different sources of data may contribute to more than one of these objectives. Historic documents might provide information regarding the presence of a site, but they would be unlikely to answer questions regarding its exact location and state of preservation, and, conversely, aerial photographs give a good idea of the extent of a site and provide, by analogy, some idea of date.

A critical statement of source data is an important element of any study, and since Binford's paper on archaeological research designs (Binford 1964) considerable emphasis has been placed on the value of an explicit statement of sources and methodology in allowing the conclusions of a project to be considered objectively. Very few of the 199 desk-based assessment reports consulted during this study contained a detailed list of sources, and data on the sources used had therefore to be gleaned from the text of the report itself. Fig 22 presents an analysis of the findings by year since 1988. In looking at these bar charts it must be remembered that most reports use more than one source, and the percentages expressed for each year in each source type thus reflect the number of reports which made use of that source.

It was found that 15% of reports produced in 1991 failed to record consultation of the SMR. Since the SMR is the fundamental source of relevance to a desk-based study it seems fair to assume that this constitutes an omission from the methods statement rather than a lack of consultation, although this assumption may be ill-founded. Our attention has been drawn to the fact that some clients feel uneasy about carrying out detailed examinations of public records such as an SMR at an early stage in the formulation of development proposals because of the commercial sensitivity of schemes at that stage in their evolution. This reluctance may in part account for the pattern recorded by the present survey. At the very least it renders uncertain the academic value of many of the assessment reports so far produced. This is all the more worrying given that previous desk-based assessments are already being used as sources for the assessment of other development proposals.

It is clear from the fact that the percentages of reports citing historic and modern literature are roughly even that there is no evidence to suggest that desk-based assessments are avoiding the less accessible types of documentation. The use of aerial photographs is restricted to those assessment projects relating to responsive types of landscape, but the broad increase in their consultation suggests an increasing recognition of their potential (Palmer and Cox 1993). Although the

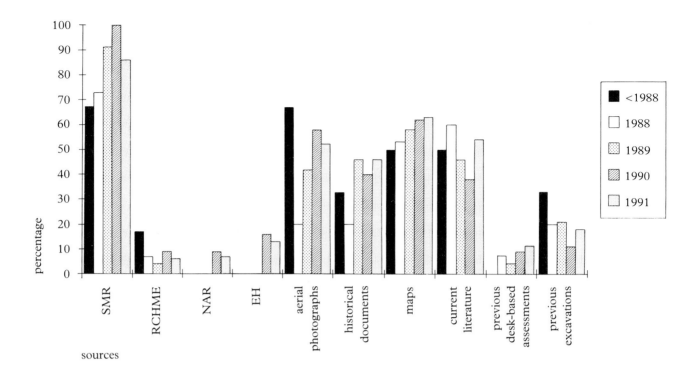

Fig 22 Sources consulted in desk-based assessments (including multiple sources consulted within a project). Shown here as a percentage of the total number of recorded desk-based assessments each year; sample size 190

percentage of desk-based assessments whose authors had consulted the English Heritage record of Scheduled Monuments showed a slight downturn in 1991, the absolute figures have risen each year. The rise in the number of Scheduled Monuments as a result of the Monuments Protection Programme must be weighed against this. One of the most inexplicable trends apparent from Fig 22 is the low percentages of projects which appear to be making use of the National Archaeological Record and the Royal Commission's county volumes (although these do not provide national coverage). In this connection it should be borne in mind that the NAR was undergoing a period of development and computerisation during the latter part of the period subject to the review (RCHME 1973, 7–8). This may have artificially depressed recorded use of the record for assessment purposes. The slight rises apparent in the absolute figures do not match the overall rate of increase in the quantity of desk-based assessments being produced.

Table 2 presents a matrix showing the frequency with which sources have been used in combination. Only two pairs can be shown on the table, although in reality some projects will draw on more than two sources. As might be expected, sources such as excavation reports and previous desk-based assessments are rarely used except in combination with inquiries of SMRs. The most numerous instance of combined sources was the consultation of an SMR and early maps (A and G), which was reported in just over 50% of assessment reports. The high incidence of literature searches and

use of aerial photography combined with SMR checks is difficult to explain, since most SMRs are (or should be) founded on the integration of information from these very sources. In general the way in which sources are combined is rather unimaginative and suggests

Table 2 Matrix summarising the coincidence of sources used in desk-based archaeological assessments (sample size = 199)

	A	B	C	D	E	F	G	H	I	J
A	–	12	12	22	89	70	106	82	15	27
B	–	–	5	5	7	6	12	7	2	4
C	–	–	–	8	7	6	9	5	3	2
D	–	–	–	–	15	14	17	7	2	2
E	–	–	–	–	–	46	71	47	5	11
F	–	–	–	–	–	–	72	46	6	12
G	–	–	–	–	–	–	–	71	9	19
H	–	–	–	–	–	–	–	–	8	13
I	–	–	–	–	–	–	–	–	–	8
J	–	–	–	–	–	–	–	–	–	–

A	SMR
B	RCHME volume
C	NAR
D	English Heritage Scheduled Monument Record
E	aerial photographic collections
F	historical documents
G	maps
H	literature search
I	previous assessments
J	excavation reports

repetition of effort, inadequacies among existing records, or a preoccupation with the validation of consolidated data sources.

The range of sources utilised by the projects investigated for this study falls short of that proposed in the draft standards for desk-based archaeological assessments issued for consultation by the Institute of Field Archaeologists (IFA 1993a).

Outcomes

Desk-based archaeological assessments are essentially works of synthesis which must rely on a number of factors if they are to reflect adequately the true archaeological potential of an area. The principal factors involved are the quantity, quality, and reliability of existing sources, the quality of the interpretations made, and the abilities and experience of those carrying out the work.

Of the 199 desk-based assessments recorded in this survey, only 12 (c 6%) revealed an absence of archaeological remains within the defined study area. Of these, one gave rise to further work to verify the finding. The relatively low number of instances where archaeology appears to be absent must in part be a reflection of the large areas which are generally covered by assessment programmes; the density of archaeological remains in Britain is such that there are few areas in which nothing will be found if a detailed search is made.

The questions to be considered, therefore, are not simply those of presence or absence but rather those of significance and importance. During the period

covered by this study only 24% of the desk-based assessment reports examined made use of the DoE criteria for the recognition of monuments of national importance (see Chapter 2, The concept of importance) nor was there evidence of the use of alternative criteria. This suggests that the archaeological resource is being managed on the basis of unstructured, subjective judgements, probably at the level only of local or county significance.

The kind of archaeology revealed

The range of archaeology revealed by synthetic studies of the kind typical of desk-based assessments partly reflects the level of existing documentation for certain periods recorded in SMRs. Table 7 compares SMR data with data recorded from desk-based assessment reports. The differences in the proportions of Roman and medieval sites are especially notable. The reallocation of undated sites in SMRs to redress the balance does not explain this discrepancy, because Roman and medieval remains are the most easily dated.

Fig 23 shows the number of sites reported for the conventionally recognised cultural/historical periods, the size of the units assigned to each period on the histogram being roughly proportional to their duration in centuries. Curiously, no Palaeolithic or Mesolithic sites were recorded from assessment projects. The figures can be seen to rise from the Neolithic period through to the end of the Roman period, which matches the expected level of visibility of sites from these periods. The Anglo-Saxon period remains one of

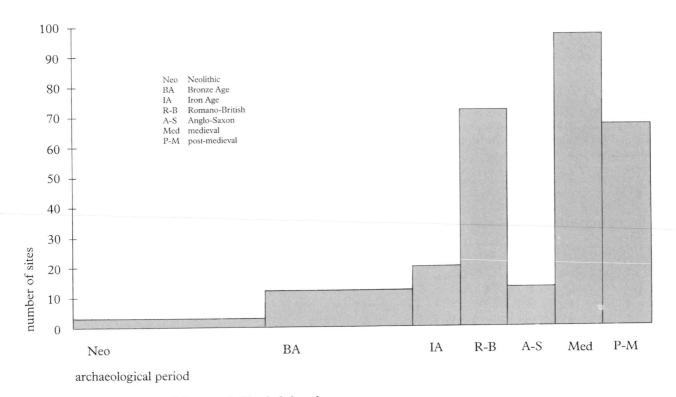

Fig 23 Total of archaeological sites revealed by desk-based assessments

the archaeologically worst-represented periods. The most highly visible period in the assessment reports examined was the medieval, with a decline in the post-medieval period. This may in part reflect the chronological limits placed on many desk-based assessments and on the data held by SMRs (RCHME 1993, 30).

Costs

The survey asked contractors and consultants to supply information about the cost and time requirements of producing desk-based assessments. It was found that costs of research and production were low compared with field evaluation. Only one desk-based assessment recorded in this study cost more than £5,000 to produce. A desk-based assessment can usually be prepared within four weeks, and many were carried out in less than three weeks. It is apparent, therefore, that desk-based assessments provide a cheap and quick means for developers and curators to discover the possible implications of archaeology in relation to planning applications, before the financial commitment of a full-scale field evaluation. Indeed, the survey recorded anecdotal evidence that a well-researched desk-based assessment can save time and money at the field evaluation stage, because the brief/specification for the field evaluation can be more precisely framed and the availability of this background information allows more accurate interpretation during recording in the field.

The integration of desk-based assessments and field evaluations

The Pagoda Report (Pagoda Projects 1992, 12) states that county archaeologists have found it easier to persuade planning officers to ask for a field evaluation before determining a planning application if the developer had already undertaken desk-based research. Nonetheless, the progression from a desk-based assessment to a field evaluation (ie site investigation) is not inevitable. The absolute number of desk-based assessments giving rise to field evaluation has increased steadily from 3 in 1988 to 65 in 1991, although the percentage of desk-based assessments which have gone on to further work has decreased steadily from 81% in 1988 to 67% in 1991 (Fig 24). There are probably two reasons for this, each typifying a different philosophy.

First, although a carefully prepared desk-based assessment is likely to record the presence of archaeological remains of some kind, the archaeology that is recorded is often judged to be of limited interest or importance and thus not worthy of further field evaluation. As the Pagoda Report (ibid, 12) shows, the

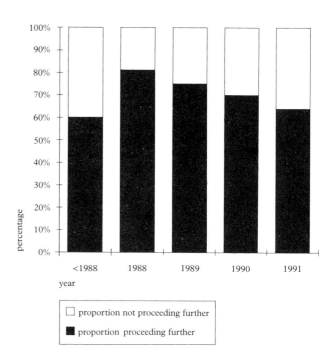

Fig 24 Percentage of recorded desk-based assessments leading to further work; sample size 191

concept of importance is sometimes coloured by the extent to which a planning authority encourages new development; and other factors extraneous to archaeology may also be at work here. Here then is the carefully calculated approach, in which the commitment of modest time and resources at an early stage can sometimes save time and expense in the long run.

The second type of strategy is represented by the increasing percentage of cases in which field evaluation is the first reported assessment exercise for a prospective development. The argument runs that the only certain way to find out about the archaeology of a site is to dig holes in it. For sites where there is little scope for mitigation except rescue excavation there is often a good case for following this line of reasoning, although it is an unsophisticated, 'throw money at the problem' kind of approach.

There can be little doubt that the use of desk-based assessments is a means of allowing developers to gauge the potential scale of archaeological input which will be required of them at the field evaluation stage and beyond. It was not possible to determine by means of this survey to what extent such information influences decisions to proceed with proposals.

The types of developments which are assessed before proceeding to an field evaluation phase may be significant. The figures for 1991 show some variation in the relationship of development types which were assessed prior to field evaluation. The most and least popular types of development site for pre-evaluation assessment are given in Table 3.

Table 3 Summary of the development types most and least frequently subject to desk-based archaeological assessments before field evaluations based on figures for 1991

development types most frequently assessed prior to evaluation		*development types least frequently assessed prior to evaluation*	
service infrastructure	(57%)	urban commercial	(13%)
pipelines	(52%)	housing estates	(13%)
road schemes	(51%)	single houses	(9%)
golf courses	(40%)	urban residential	(7%)
green field sites	(30%)	housing extension	(6%)

One of the most striking points to emerge from Table 3 is the scale of the development types using desk-based assessment before field evaluation. The top three (service infrastructure, pipelines, and road schemes) are also among those development types which move most slowly through the planning process, presumably allowing time for a phased response to archaeology. The incidence of golf courses may be explained by the policy of some curators to request an assessment only if those parts of the golf course where groundworks will be required cannot be kept away from areas of known or potential archaeological sensitivity. The development types least likely to be assessed prior to field evaluation are privately funded projects whose promoters are usually operating on a short time-scale.

Field evaluations

How many, where, and when?

The survey recorded a total of 1333 field evaluations carried out between 1982 and 1991. This total includes examples of investigations carried out before 1988 which may not have been called field evaluations but fulfilled the same purposes and were carried out within comparable parameters.

Fig 25 shows the rise in the number of field evaluations carried out over the period of the survey, with the greatest increases (63%) occurring in the north between 1990 and 1991 following the introduction of PPG 16. The general trend, however, stems from much earlier.

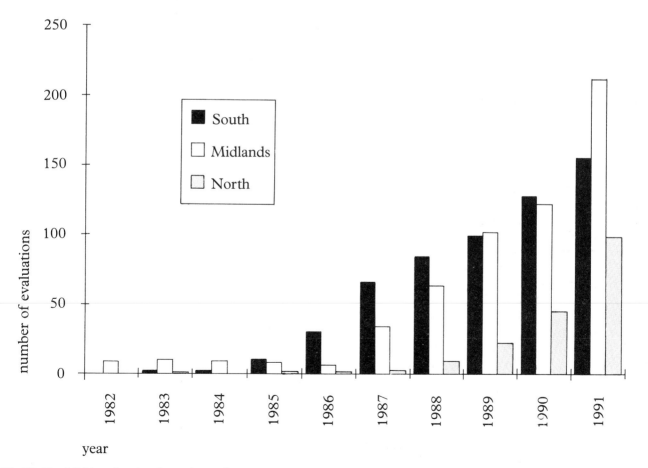

Fig 25 Total field evaluations by region and year

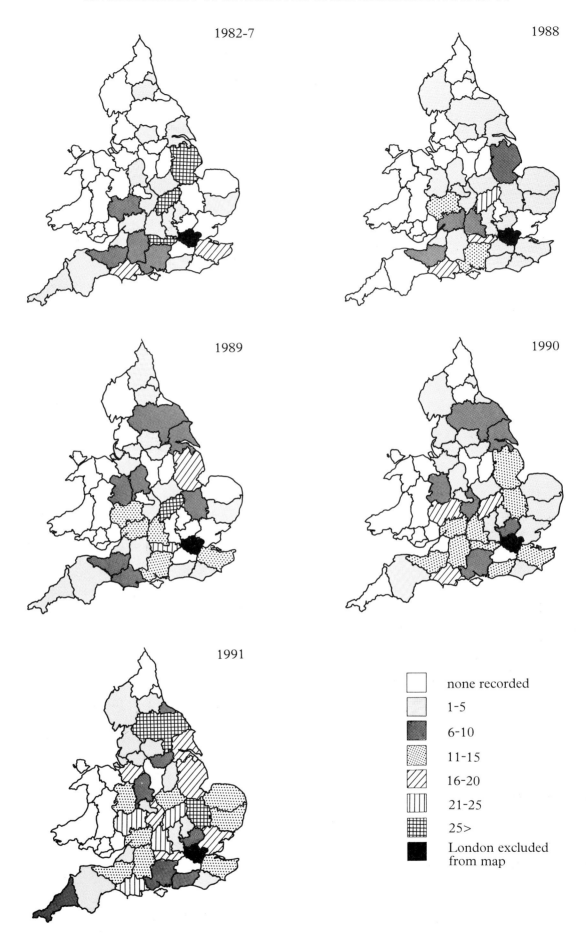

Fig 26 Geographical distribution of field evaluation projects by county and year

Until 1991, the greatest number of field evaluations took place in the South region, which also saw the earliest sustained growth in the application of field evaluation. In 1991 the greatest number was in the Midlands, where the earliest cases recorded in the survey were found. The first report falling within the modern definition of pre-planning response was completed in Hereford and Worcester in 1982. As a whole, the Midland counties show an interesting minor peak around 1983, perhaps the result of the way in which MSC archaeology programmes were deployed in the area. Northern counties become involved in field evaluation later, undoubtedly reflecting the changing patterns of regional development which are also visible in the number of recorded planning applications (see Chapter 3, Introduction).

This regional picture is, however, only a simplification of the more complicated pattern of evolution and spread of field evaluations which can be seen on Fig 26. On this series of maps it can be seen that up to 1988 the majority of field evaluations took place in South Western, central Southern, and Midland counties. Over the succeeding years the distribution and spread of assessment have covered most of the country.

It is interesting to note that although the number of planning applications with an archaeological dimension has levelled off or is in decline in most parts of the country, the number of field evaluations is still rising. This presumably reflects a change in the types of responses employed by curators towards the pre-planning field evaluation of sites advocated by PPG 16.

The basis of selection and brief setting

In ideal circumstances the decision to evaluate a given site or area might be regarded as inevitably dependent on the results of earlier work such as desk-based assessment. However, the assessment phase is often bypassed because time is not available or there is already a high level of knowledge regarding a site (and see Chapter 5, The integration of desk-based assessments and field evaluations).

Very few sites are subject to field evaluation unless there is known archaeology either on or adjacent to the development area ie within about 200m. Overall there was known archaeology on more than 60% of sites before field evaluation (see Figs 27a and 27b), but the percentage varies from a minimum of 40% in the North in 1990 to a maximum of 100% in the North in 1988. This figure does not decrease consistently as the number of field evaluations increases and one reason for this may be the increased priority given to archaeological considerations within the planning system. It is possible that as a result of this more marginal sites are being evaluated, or that curators are better placed to request field evaluation, instead of responding to the presence of archaeology by recommending that a condition be added to the planning consent. There is a related possibility that the definition of what constitutes significant archaeology has changed, and that sites which would have been insignificant in the early 1980s are now considered worth evaluating.

Fig 28 shows an analysis of the prompts that brought about field evaluation programmes. The fairly consistent level of voluntary efforts is notable, the influence of PPG 16 since 1990 predictable. Local structure plan policies are most frequently cited as the basis on which work is justified.

As with desk-based assessments, it might be expected that the presence of Scheduled Ancient Monuments would be a significant factor in prompting projects. The survey revealed that the proportion of study areas containing SAMs has fallen from c 11% before 1988 to c 7% in 1991. This presumably reflects a tendency towards the preservation of nationally important archaeological sites and their settings,

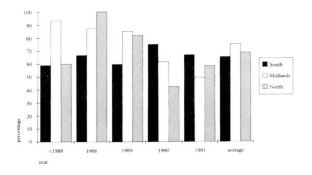

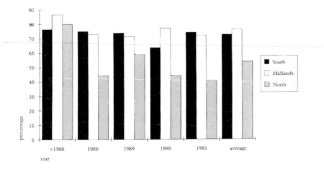

Fig 27 Percentage of field evaluation by region conducted where there was an existing level of archaeological awareness of (top) on-site archaeology, sample size 1021, and (bottom) adjacent archaeology, sample size 1021

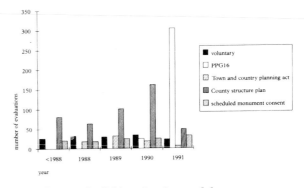

Fig 28 Prompt for field evaluation work by year

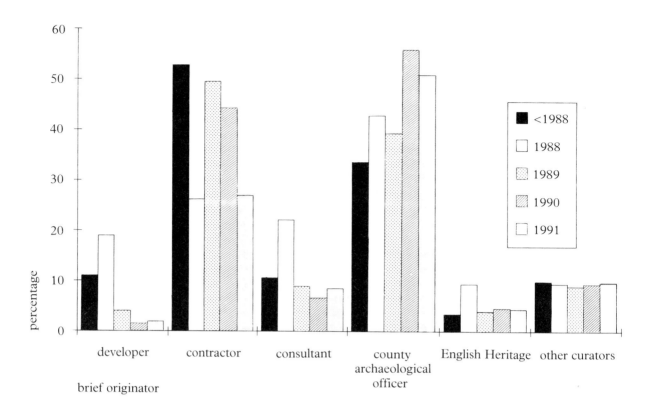

Fig 29 Authors of field evaluation briefs as a percentage of the total recorded field evaluations each year, (top) South region, sample size 509, (bottom) Midlands region, sample size 395, and North region (overleaf top), sample size 143

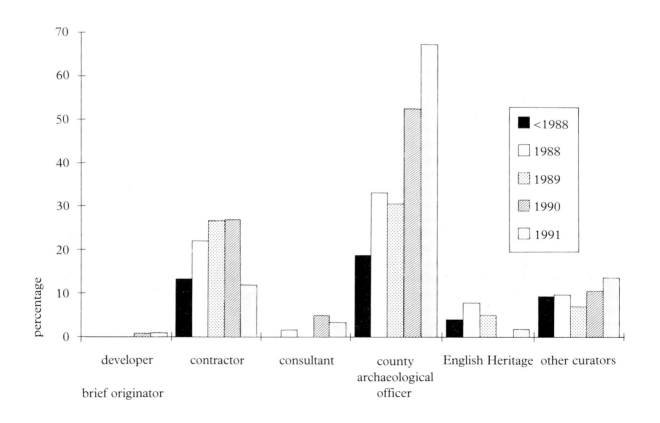

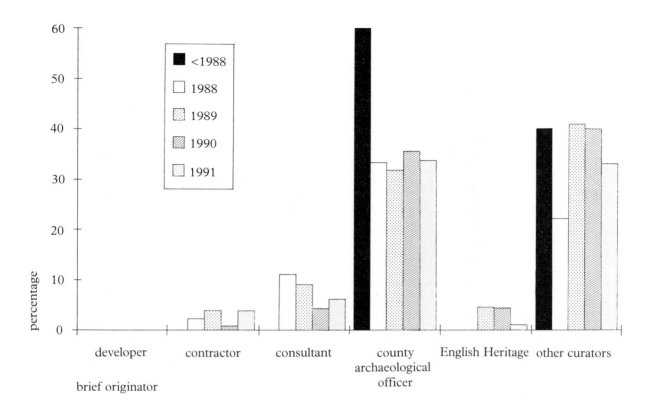

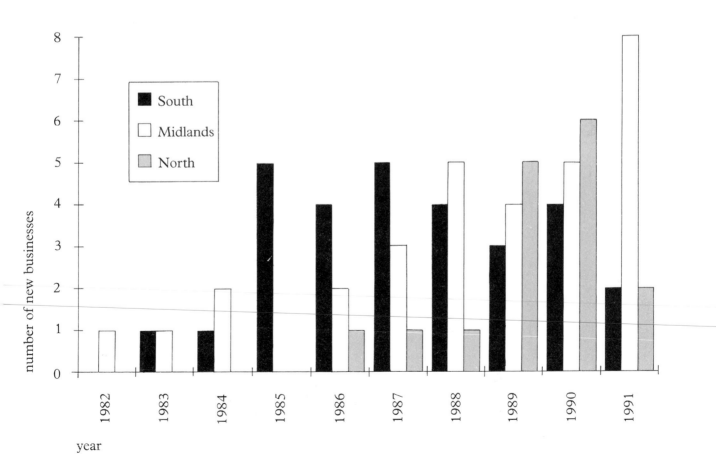

Fig 30 Number of new businesses entering into field evaluation work each year

whether or not they are scheduled (DoE 1991, paragraph 8).

The survey included briefs and specifications, recognising that the scope and quality of such documents has only recently been identified as a major issue (ACAO 1993) and that because of this the data for the period before 1989 can be regarded only as indicative. Model briefs have been issued for London (English Heritage 1992 a and 1992 b) and a number of county archaeological officers now provide guidelines on field evaluation procedures and expected standards. A draft standard on field evaluation has been set out by the IFA (1993b). Fig 29 provides an analysis by region of those responsible for preparing briefs and specifications. The early dominance of contractors undertaking design-and-execute programmes is notable, a practice overtaken but not replaced in more recent years by briefs issued by curators. The Southampton project has addressed the question of briefs and specifications in more detail with an analysis covering the period 1988–92 (Champion et al 1995).

Who does the work?

Archaeological contractors now undertake most field evaluations, although at the time of the survey a number of contractors were effectively part of organisations which also had a curatorial role.

Since 1985 there has been an upward trend in the number of new contractors undertaking field evaluation work throughout England (Fig 30). Before 1985 the numbers fluctuated between none and two in each of the three regions, reflecting the *ad hoc* nature of the field evaluation process at that time. All three regions have experienced a fall-off in the total number of businesses operating within them between 1988 and 1990 (the South in 1988, and the Midlands and North in 1989). In the South and Midlands this was due to a fall in the number of new businesses and the disappearance of existing firms. In the North, this decline is more difficult to interpret, because although existing firms moved out of field evaluation work there is no evidence

to suggest a fall in the number of new businesses entering into field evaluations. A similar depression can be seen in the total number of businesses carrying out assessment work in 1988–9.

After 1989 the exponential increase in the number of new businesses was maintained only in the Midlands (eight in 1991; only those contractors with a home base in the Midlands were counted), and this is reflected in the large number of firms which operated in this area in 1991. In the south and north of the country the numbers of businesses operating continue to increase but at a slower rate, presumably reflecting saturation in the market for new firms, or an expansion in the scale of existing firms.

Background data

In any field evaluation project it is necessary to consult a range of sources in order to target areas for work and provide context and background. In some cases this was achieved as part of a desk-based assessment, but in *c* 10% of field evaluations this exercise was included within the field evaluation itself. Table 4 shows the range of sources used in studies of this kind. Although the percentage use of all the main sources has increased over the course of time the reliance placed on sources has remained remarkably consistent. Interestingly, despite the increase in the number of free-standing desk-based archaeological assessments, the number of such studies included within field evaluation reports has not decreased and actually increased in the South and Midlands in 1991. Nonetheless, these reports fulfil the same roles as a separate assessment, being used for the identification of areas of potential, and are not designed for the active definition of sites for field evaluation.

Size of the field evaluation area

Since field evaluations focus on specific sites (ie land units) rather than on general development areas it is not surprising that different patterns should be seen in the

Table 4   The incidence of background data source types used in field evaluation projects by year

	A	B	C	D	E	F	G	H	I	J	K
<1988	44.0%	0.6%	0%	2.6%	1.9%	2.6%	1.3%	11.9%	7.9%	26.0%	1.1%
1988	44.0%	2.2%	0.7%	2.2%	4.5%	1.5%	3.7%	11.2%	11.2%	18.0%	0.8%
1989	42.0%	0%	0.3%	0.3%	1.1%	1.9%	1.9%	13.3%	9.1%	19.5%	10.6%
1990	39.0%	1.0%	0%	1.3%	1.6%	1.6%	1.3%	15.7%	11.4%	16.5%	10.6%
1991	49.0%	0.5%	0%	1.1%	3.5%	3.5%	1.3%	14.7%	12.2%	13.6%	0.6%

A	SMR	G	maps
B	RCHME volume	H	literature search
C	NAR	I	previous assessments
D	English Heritage Scheduled Monument Record	J	excavation reports
E	aerial photographic collections	K	other minor sources
F	historical documents		

size of areas covered by desk-based assessments as opposed to field evaluations. It is clear that the size of the possible archaeological site rather than of the development site is the important factor. This was discussed in Chapter 4, Land-use in the development area, with the conclusion that in the north of the country there is a bias towards areas of less than 1ha. This is probably a factor of the size of the development areas rather than a reflection of the size of archaeological sites in the North region. Over the rest of the country roughly equal numbers of small, medium, and large areas were subject to field evaluation. It is assumed that in practice many of the large areas each encompassed a number of more or less separate archaeological sites or features within the single field evaluation project.

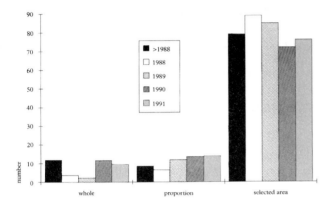

Fig 31 Proportion of a study area selected for field evaluation

Fig 31 examines the relationship between the area of development sites subject to field evaluation and the proportion of the area actually evaluated. Three categories were used to judge this relationship, the whole area available, a part of the site (eg northern half only), or specially selected and therefore highly sensitive areas within the site (eg only where archaeological features were already known). As can be seen, the field evaluation of whole sites had an early period of popularity, then became unusual, and in recent years has again been more widely applied. Over the same period the practice of examining a proportion of the development site has generally increased while the highly selective field evaluation of special areas has decreased. These changes are undoubtedly connected with the introduction of PPG 16 as a prompt for extensive field evaluations.

Techniques and procedures of investigation

The survey revealed that there is considerable divergence of opinion throughout the country concerning the 'best' way of approaching a field evaluation. Time and cost are strong constraints (as they are in any other area of archaeology), but there is also the practical problem posed by the availability of windows of opportunity in, for example, the agricultural cycle, during which techniques such as fieldwalking can be deployed. It is unusual for a site to remain available for evaluation throughout an entire year, allowing the contractor to select opportune times to practise different techniques.

It might be expected that one way of overcoming the problems of timing would be to undertake a field evaluation in stages. The survey revealed, however, that only *c* 9% of field evaluations have been carried out in more than one phase.

Detailed information about the methods employed was available for 1035 out of the 1333 field evaluations recorded. Table 5 provides an analysis of the incidence of various techniques deployed; Fig 32 presents an analysis of technique deployment by region. In looking at these figures it must be remembered that in some cases more than one technique was deployed in a given study.

Table 5   Summary of the deployment of various archaeological techniques in field evaluations 1982-91 (based on 1035 projects with data on methods)

technique	incidence	% of evaluations in which this method was used alone or in combination with other methods
target trenches	565	54.5%
random trenches	335	32.3%
test pits	167	16.1%
documentary searches	131	12.6%
fieldwalking	123	11.8%
magnetometry	112	10.8%
topographic survey	73	7.0%
resistivity	59	5.7%
aerial photography	22	2.1%
auger survey	12	1.1%
ground probing radar	11	1.0%
magnetic susceptibility	7	0.6%
phosphate studies	4	0.3%
metal detector survey	3	0.2%

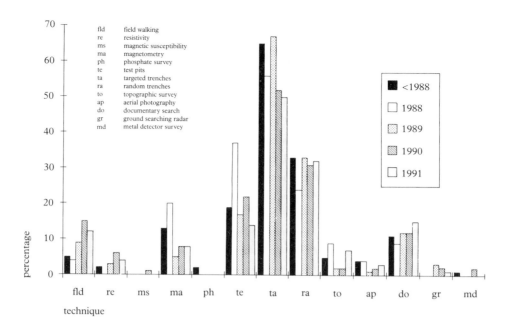

Fig 32 Techniques employed in field evaluation work by region as a percentage of that region's total number of recorded field evaluations each year in (top) South region, sample size 533, (below) Midlands region, sample size 359, and (overleaf top) North region, sample size 146

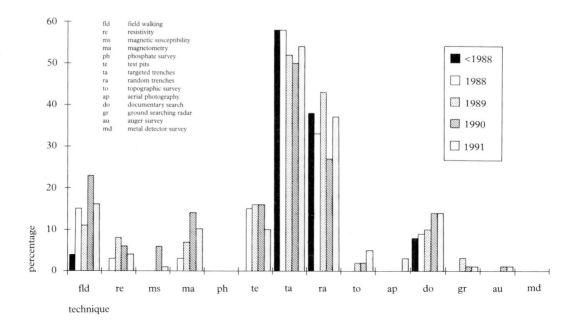

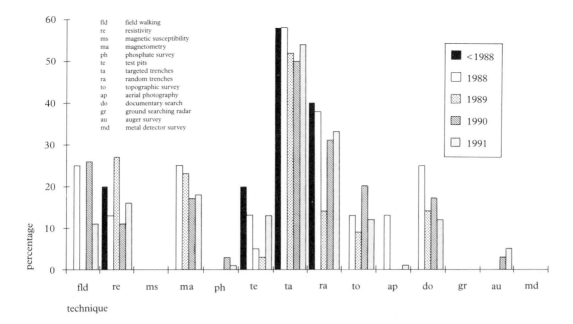

fld field walking
re resistivity
ms magnetic susceptibility
ma magnetometry
ph phosphate survey
te test pits
ta targeted trenches
ra random trenches
to topographic survey
ap aerial photography
do documentary search
gr ground searching radar
au auger survey
md metal detector survey

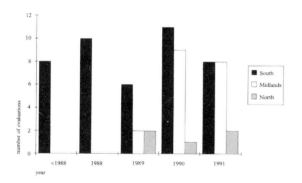

Fig 33 Number of field evaluations using test-pits and trenches each year

Fieldwalking is favoured on sites greater than 20ha, and is used primarily in the South and Midlands regions, reflecting the greater percentages of arable land in these areas than in the North. This distribution also reflects variations in the popularity of this technique and the confidence placed in it by different curators when writing their briefs. Some curators requested fieldwalking in all relevant situations. It was found to have been used in 11.8% of all field evaluations investigated. In the case of some staged field evaluations, later phases built on the evidence of this early work.

Magnetometry is the most popular of the geophysical techniques, especially on rural sites, presumably because of the speed with which the technique can be used over large areas. Resistivity is also widely used. Both techniques are more commonly used in the north of the country, possibly because the major geophysical sub-contractor was based in this part of England during the time covered by our survey. In the South and Midlands there is a slight decrease in the use of these techniques, matched by the rise in single phase random trenching.

Test-pitting (small, regularly placed holes used to investigate sub-surface deposits and quantify deposit content in the case of topsoil studies) appears to be used in two different circumstances, firstly on small sites (less than 1ha) where there may be insufficient space to position trenches, and secondly on very large sites, where it can serve a useful role in the recognition of sites which are far apart. As a technique it is favoured in the south of the country, again perhaps reflecting curator confidence, although it is decreasing in popularity compared to random trenching.

Random trenching is deployed on 32.3% of field evaluations and is widely regarded as the best technique available in cases where little or nothing is known about archaeological deposits in the field evaluation area. There is little evidence that the placing of trenches is based on the application of statistically meaningful sampling strategies; instead, professional judgement seems to be the guiding factor, and the idea of randomness may need qualification.

The single most widely deployed method is targeted trenching, which was applied in about 54.5% of recorded field evaluations. This technique involves the examination of definite and possible features and deposits detected from existing records (eg transcriptions of aerial photographs), geophysical survey or fieldwalking. Since 1989 there has been a trend towards the combination of test-pits and trenches as part of an integrated field evaluation strategy (Fig 33). The Southampton project carried out a more detailed analysis of the relationship between test-pitting and trial trenching with reference to Hampshire and Berkshire (Champion et al 1995).

Existing aerial photographs are regarded as a source of background data, but a few cases were noted where new aerial coverage was specially commissioned as part of the field evaluation exercise.

Topographic surveys were rarely deployed during field evaluations, although analytical surveys of

Table 6   Matrix summarising the coincidence of methods used in field evaluation (based on sample of 1035 projects with data on method used)

	A	B	C	D	E	F	G	H	J	K	L	M	N	O
A	25	5	2	23	0	25	48	25	21	8	25	2	1	3
B	-	9	1	15	1	10	35	6	3	0	8	0	1	0
C	-	-	2	2	0	1	2	2	0	0	0	0	0	0
D	-	-	-	9	2	43	50	8	19	3	17	0	1	0
E	-	-	-	-	0	2	1	3	1	0	1	0	0	0
F	-	-	-	-	-	34	63	32	15	5	13	2	3	0
G	-	-	-	-	-	-	319	40	36	14	76	6	2	3
H	-	-	-	-	-	-	-	226	8	3	20	0	5	0
J	-	-	-	-	-	-	-	-	6	12	33	2	0	0
K	-	-	-	-	-	-	-	-	-	0	15	1	0	0
L	-	-	-	-	-	-	-	-	-	-	3	5	0	0
M	-	-	-	-	-	-	-	-	-	-	-	0	0	0
N	-	-	-	-	-	-	-	-	-	-	-	-	4	0
O	-	-	-	-	-	-	-	-	-	-	-	-	-	0

A	*fieldwalking*	H	*random trenches*
B	*resistivity*	J	*topographic surveys*
C	*magnetic susceptibility*	K	*aerial photography*
D	*magnetometry*	L	*documentary sources*
E	*phosphate studies*	M	*ground probing radar*
F	*test pits*	N	*auger surveys*
G	*targeted trenches*	O	*metal detector surveys*

NB *Diagonal axis shows single method only cases*

standing earthworks, however slight, can be important where appropriate. Techniques such as ground probing radar and augering are rarely used.

Fieldwalking, geophysics, and to a lesser extent test-pitting can be seen as preliminary phases of investigation which are used to inform decisions on trench location, since in most cases it is only through excavation that questions relating to the quality of preserved archaeology can be answered. As we have already stated, however, pressure of time often means that these techniques are used in the same phase of work, limiting the level of interpretation possible before trenches are placed. It must also be noted that, in broad terms, the different techniques can be seen as having different values for field evaluation, depending on the extent to which they provide data which inform the questions of importance and significance. For example, fieldwalking gives a broad idea of the parameters of some types of sites but no idea of the extent or quality of subsoil features, and geophysics can provide the evidence for subsoil features but cannot answer questions relating to the nature, date, or quality of those features.

The survey investigated the way in which techniques were combined. Between 60% and 70% of the field evaluation reports examined referred to projects which used only one method of investigation. This figure is, however, somewhat imprecise, and is probably inflated slightly by the fact that when projects were broken into phases the reports dealt with only one phase at a time. Approximately 24% of field evaluation projects used two methods, 9.5% three methods, 4% drew on the results of four methods, and less than 2% of the studies reviewed used five methods.

The combinations of methods which were deployed are perhaps of more interest than the number of separate methods used. The nature of phased projects again makes precise analysis difficult, but Table 6 shows the results of a simple comparison of the links and connections between pairs of techniques. It is clear from this that only some methods are used in isolation (notably trenching of various kinds), whereas certain combinations such as fieldwalking and targeted trenching, geophysical survey and targeted trenching, and documentary research and targeted trenching are widely used.

The range of techniques which archaeologists are using in field evaluations seems to be decreasing through time in all areas (Fig 32). Greater emphasis is being placed on a more restricted range of methods. This appears to be part of a general problem, stemming from the lack of research into the effectiveness of different techniques in field evaluation. It is also notable that most of the techniques deployed have been carried over in a relatively unmodified form from research-oriented archaeology. No techniques seem to have been developed with the special problems posed by field evaluation for archaeological resource management in mind. This is a deficiency which could perhaps be addressed by the major research councils, in particular by SBAC.

Field evaluation results

For the purposes of comparison it is assumed that all the field evaluations recorded had a true result, in the sense that the diagnosis of the nature and extent of any

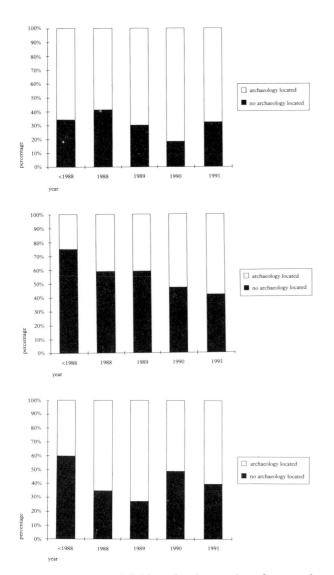

Fig 34 Outcomes of field evaluation projects by year in (top) South region, (middle) Midlands region, and (bottom) North region

archaeology present was correct (whether positive or negative). No attempt has been made to check the validity of stated diagnoses in the light of subsequent work on the site. However, the Southampton project examined six cases in Hampshire and Berkshire where field evaluation led to further excavation, and concluded that in only one instance were the results significantly different (Champion *et al* 1995).

Fig 34 shows an analysis by region of the distribution of field evaluation results in terms of a positive or negative outcome (ie whether archaeological deposits were encountered or not). The percentage of field evaluations in 1991 which revealed no archaeological deposits (true negative) was *c* 38%. Table 8 summarises the outcomes of all field evaluation programmes recorded in the survey and compares them with the presence or absence of known archaeology before the field evaluation. Four possible patterns are defined. It is notable that although 44% of field evaluations effectively confirmed the presence of archaeological deposits (true positive outcome in situations where archaeology was previously recorded on site), some 31.2% of field evaluations yielded a true negative despite the fact that there were previous records of archaeological remains on the site. This figure may call into question the assumption that all the recorded field evaluations had true outcomes, although the acceptance of the likelihood that some had false outcomes cannot explain only one row of figures on the table, because in that case all the figures would be affected. The observation that 17.3% of evaluations revealed a true positive outcome when previous records would have led one to expect a true negative must be balanced against this. All this highlights the need for direct intervention through field evaluation rather than reliance on an existing record concerning the supposed state of preservation of a site. The question of the extent to which SMRs can be used as predictive tools is addressed by the Southampton project.

Fig 34 also reveals some regional differences in the proportion of field evaluations identifying an absence of archaeological deposits and a general trend of decline in the proportion of field evaluations revealing an absence of archaeology from 1988 to 1990. Two explanations of this decline may be offered. In the first place, it may be that field evaluation methodologies were improving and hence that diagnoses were becoming more accurate. Secondly, it may be that the selection of sites for field evaluation became more rigorous, and that it was increasingly the case that only those sites considered most likely to contain archaeological deposits were selected for field evaluation. The reality probably involves an element of both explanations, although the second is perhaps more important if the reversal of the

Table 7 Comparison of sites recorded by period in county SMRs, desk-based archaeological assessments, and field evaluations

archaeological period	percentage of sites by period recorded nationally by SMRs (data based on IAM 1984)	percentage of sites by period recorded by archaeological assessment	percentage of sites by period recorded by field evaluation
prehistoric	27.6	21.9	20.4
Romano-British	11.1	22.6	23.9
early medieval	3.0	4.1	4.9
medieval	20.6	30.4	29.8
post-medieval	23.3	21.0	21.0
uncertain date	14.4	–	–

Table 8 Summary of field evaluation outcomes compared with the presence or absence of archaeology previously recorded on site

archaeology already recorded on site	archaeology revealed by evaluation (outcome)	percentage of total projects (sample size 1333)
yes	yes (true positive)	44.0%
yes	no (false positive)	31.2%
no	no (true negative)	7.3%
no	yes (false negative)	17.3%

trend in 1991 is attributed to the effect of greater powers available to curators after the publication of PPG 16.

The kind of archaeology revealed

The range of archaeological sites by period which have been identified in field evaluations broadly matches the pattern shown by desk-based assessments (Table 7) but matches the distribution of data recorded by SMRs only in general terms.

Fig 35 shows the chronological spread of finds from field evaluations and helps to clarify the picture for the prehistoric periods in particular. It is notable that the number of Iron Age sites located by field evaluations is greater than those found during desk-based

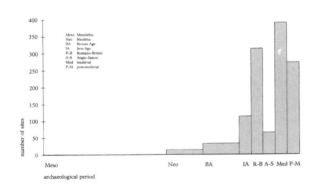

Fig 35 Total archaeological sites revealed by field evaluation

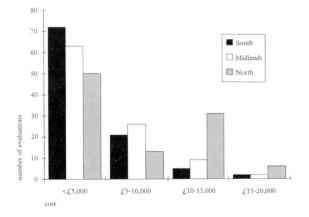

Fig 36 Costs of field evaluation projects

assessments and seems to reflect better the archaeological visibility which one would expect from this period. The low number of post-medieval sites presumably reflects the fact that in many cases this type of archaeology is represented by standing buildings, which fell outside the brief for this project.

The cost of field evaluation work

The survey asked contractors and curators to identify the approximate cost of field evaluation programmes. Fig 36 shows an analysis by region of costs for a sample of 118 field evaluations for which data were available. Nearly 90% of field evaluations cost less than £10,000, and only one project in the sample cost over £20,000. The majority of projects cost less than £5,000.

The product of desk-based assessments and field evaluations

Readership

Since 1989 it has become accepted as best practice to package the results of a desk-based assessment or field evaluation in the form of a single report. The nature and content of these reports are not standardised and there are considerable variations in both content and style throughout the country. The IFA has recently issued draft standards, including a report content scheme, for desk-based studies (ie desk-based archaeological assessments) and field evaluations (IFA 1993a; 1993b).

Two groups can be identified as constituting the primary audience of assessment reports, developers (ie clients, but including other members of project teams) and archaeological curators. A secondary audience can also be identified, comprising archaeologists (academic as well as those involved with archaeological resource management), interested third parties (eg objectors to development proposals, pressure groups, etc), and the general public.

The developer and the members of a project team (eg architects, engineers, etc) often approach the archaeological contractor with little or no experience of archaeology, and it is therefore necessary for reports to contain background information as well as a clear explanation of why the work was undertaken and what the conclusions and implications might be. The curator, on the other hand, needs a body of objective evidence on which to base an appraisal of the value of the site.

In addition to these dual requirements, the report will serve a third, academic role when it is deposited with the SMR and enters the public domain, as the only documentation which is likely to be produced for a given investigation. This is not to suggest that a report should contain major background research into the area or wider significance of the site (although these should be implicit in the county archaeologist's consideration of the site's value). It is most difficult for a field evaluation report to fulfil this third role, since field evaluation is designed to answer specific questions relating to preservation rather than to interpret the past.

The different weighting which contractors throughout the country have given to the potential readership of their reports partially influences their presentation and content. The county archaeologist who sets the brief also influences the style adopted by different units, since some curators state explicitly that the contractor must not make recommendations concerning the value of the site or further avenues of work.

At present the adequacy of a report is judged by the curator, who writes the initial brief, makes recommendations to the developer concerning the best specification received, and monitors the field evaluation. Once the field evaluation has been completed much of the context of the project is lost, and the reasons for choosing a particular field evaluation strategy, as well as the extent to which this strategy was followed, are forgotten. Replication of field evaluation is impossible where invasive techniques have been used.

Fieldwalking which involves the collection and removal of artifacts must be regarded as an invasive technique in this context. Field surveys which involve the sampling of a field surface by visual inspection without the removal of finds are not invasive. In drawing up field evaluation specifications it is sometimes appropriate to consider what kind of sampling strategy might be used at some later date, for example in recording an area if permission for development were granted. Extensive sampling at one stage may limit the available choices of sampling strategies for later deployment. The same care applies to considering what could be preserved after field evaluation and what the effect of the evaluation on the preserved resource will be. During the study, one field evaluation was found to have examined through excavation nearly all the feature intersections on the site, thus significantly reducing the stratigraphic integrity of the sections potentially available for preservation.

If the archaeological profession is to be able to judge the validity of an archaeological report and the effectiveness of the participants within the project then it is necessary to include the brief and specification within the final report, a practice already followed by some units.

It would also be valuable if the final decision on the development proposals for a site were to be lodged in the SMR at the end of the planning process. If the academic value of a site appears to warrant further research at a later date the complete investigative history of the site can then be examined in one place, instead of being in the hands of the various bodies which currently control pieces of information about a development and its archaeological potential.

Disseminating the report

The question of confidentiality of reports and the process of access has aroused considerable debate. It has become generally accepted that the report should be lodged in the SMR within six months of the completion of the assessment exercise, and several county archaeologists write this into their briefs. Nonetheless, in some cases there is still confusion over whether the deposition of material in the SMR constitutes its entry into the public domain, or whether reports are lodged there only to inform future planning decisions. Questions like these obviously warrant consideration by the profession.

The pattern of other locations in which reports are deposited is also very erratic. The survey examined the extent to which copies of reports were deposited in major libraries and found very little evidence of such deposition. In addition, few units deposit paper or fiche copies of reports with the NAR and the general response to queries on this point was that the units were not aware of the procedure of deposition and were uncertain of the accessibility of material thus submitted.

The only other outlets which are used consistently for information concerning field evaluations are the regional CBA volumes, the Annual Report (if any) of the particular unit involved, and those county journals which include 'round-ups' of recent work. Particularly useful examples recorded during this survey include those in *Transactions of the Bristol and Gloucestershire Archaeological Society* (assembled by the Committee for Archaeology in Gloucestershire), *Proceedings of the Somerset Archaeological Natural History Society* (assembled by the County Archaeological Office), and the *Wiltshire Archaeological Magazine*. For the most part this information takes the form of short summaries concerning the range of archaeology revealed by the project and the name of its funding body.

Unfortunately, the pace of work on field evaluation programmes and the high turnover of projects rarely allow time for further work on a project past the completion of the report, and journal publication including relevant specialist reports is an option which very few units are in a position to take up. Most county journals have only restricted space for excavation reports and very few field evaluations are important enough to warrant an article in a period journal.

6 Environmental assessments to 1991

Archaeology in environmental assessments

Environmental assessment, unlike either desk-based assessment or field evaluation, is a procedure established by statute. The environmental assessment is a technique for ensuring that the likely effects of new development on the environment are fully understood and taken into account before the development is allowed to go ahead. The results of environmental assessments are communicated through an environmental statement which represents the main evidence for the execution of environmental assessment projects. The term Environmental Impact Assessment is sometimes, wrongly, applied to such studies in Britain. The term is the one current in America under the US National Policy Act 1969.

The starting point for legislation in the UK is an EC Directive entitled 'The assessment of the effects of certain public and private projects on the environment' (85/337/EEC) which was adopted on 27th June 1985. The Directive was given legal effect in the UK through the *Town and Country Planning (Assessment of Environmental Effects) Regulations 1988* (SI 1199), which came into force on 15th July 1988. The procedures for determining whether a project should be subject to an environmental assessment are complicated and are summarised in a guide published by the Department of the Environment (DoE 1989). A study of the implementation of the procedures has already been undertaken (Wood and Jones 1991).

Archaeology is one of the subjects mentioned in the original EC Directive under the theme of material assets (Annex III paragraph 3), although in the UK Government's interpretation of the Directive the list of subject areas for consideration does not mention archaeology specifically, preferring the general terms 'material assets' and 'cultural heritage'.

How many studies, where, and when?

Between the coming into effect of the legislation and the end of 1991 it is estimated that some 600 environmental assessments had been carried out in England (information from the Institute of Environmental Assessment). This number had risen to about 1300 for the UK as a whole by the end of 1992 (Heaney and Therivel 1993).

Copies of about 350 of the 600 environmental statements relevant to the present study have been located, mainly at the Institute of Environmental Assessment based in East Kirkby. Out of the 350 studied, approximately 147 (42%) were found to

contain a section relating to archaeology or closely related matters (ie material assets or cultural heritage.which included archaeology. Since not all developments necessarily have a projected impact on archaeological remains the level of attention to archaeology is interesting. The sample of 147 environmental statements examined forms the basis of the quantifications presented in the remaining paragraphs of this section.

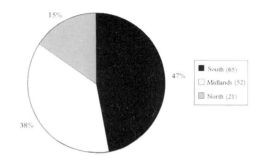

Fig 37 Percentage of recorded environmental assessments with an archaeological element by region

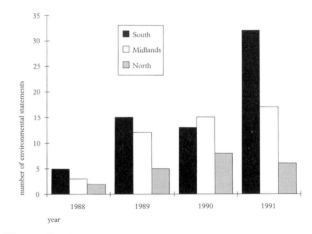

Fig 38 Total recorded environmental assessments with an archaeological element by region and year

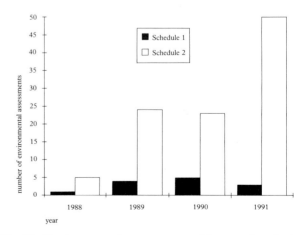

Fig 39 Environmental assessments with an archaeological element in Schedule 1 or 2 by year

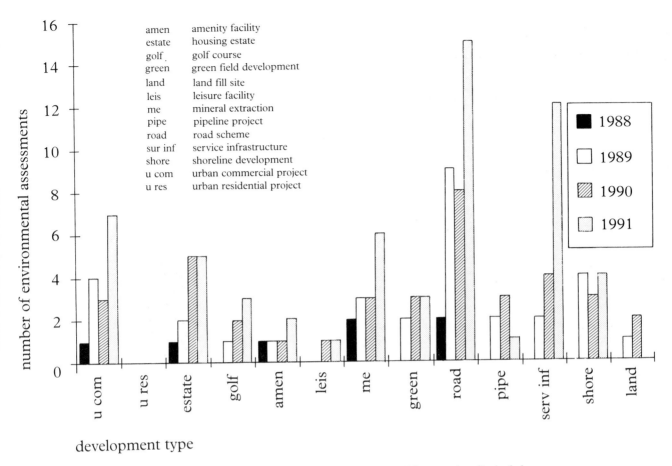

Fig 40 Development types prompting recorded environmental assessments with an archaeological element

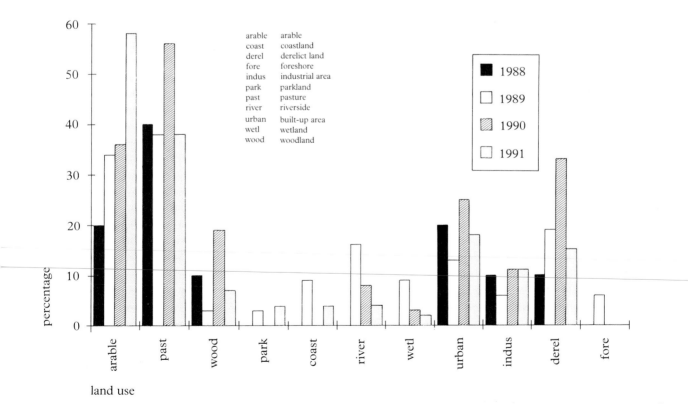

Fig 41 Land-use types from the archaeological study area as a percentage of the total recorded environmental assessments each year, sample size 124

Fig 37 shows the overall distribution of environmental statements containing an archaeological element by region, emphasising the relatively large number from the South and Midland regions by comparison with the North. Fig 38 shows the growth in the number of statements produced by region, from which it can be seen that in the South and Midland regions the upward trend appears to be continuing, whereas in the North there is a slight decline in the number completed in 1991.

The legislation specifies the kinds of project which may be subject to environmental assessment and divides them into two groups. For Schedule 1 projects environmental assessment is mandatory (these are highly sensitive projects such as nuclear power stations), and for Schedule 2 projects such an assessment is discretionary on the basis of guidelines issued by the Department of the Environment. Fig 39 shows an analysis of the two main groups of project in which archaeology was included as part of the analysis. As might be expected, the number of Schedule 1 projects is relatively small and has remained stable at fewer than five examples per year. Most of the overall rise in the number of environmental assessments carried out is accounted for by Schedule 2 projects, which show a steady year by year rise.

Fig 40 looks in more detail at the kinds of development which have given rise to environmental statements with an archaeological component. Among these, road and infrastructure schemes stand out as dominant, especially in 1991. This reflects a general pattern in which 33% of environmental assessment projects were related to infrastructure work (Wood and Jones 1991, 8).

These developments occur most frequently on pasture and arable land (Fig 41), although built-up land, industrial land, and derelict land are also well-represented land-use types. It is notable that the size of area subject to environmental assessment has increased as the technique has become more widely applied. Fig 42 presents an analysis of the data, from which the growth of environmental assessments on large sites

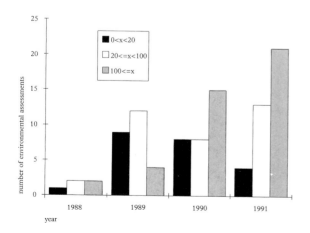

Fig 42 Size of the archaeological area within recorded environmental assessments

(over 100ha) is very clear. Given that environmental assessment is intended to deal with developments which are likely to have substantial effects this is not unexpected.

Who does the work?

The survey recorded the number of businesses in each of the three regions which were carrying out environmental assessments with archaeological components. Fig 43 presents a summary analysis of the changing pattern through time. Comparison of this pattern with the total number of assessments being carried out (Fig 38) suggests that in the South there was a relatively high number of firms each of which carried out a high number of assessments, that in the Midlands there was also a relatively large number of firms each of which carried out a few assessments, and that in the North small numbers of firms were turning over small numbers of assessments. Some of the assessments in the North region must have been carried out by firms based elsewhere, perhaps in the Midlands.

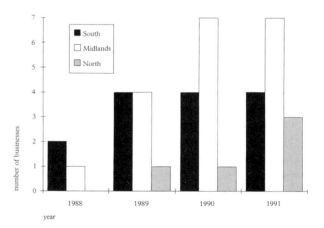

Fig 43 Total archaeological businesses working on recorded environmental assessments each year

The archaeological sections of the statements examined were checked to see who carried out the investigations and prepared the reports. The work was categorised as being that of a recognised archaeologist/ archaeological organisation or that of a non-archaeologist/non-archaeological organisation. The basis for assigning reports to these categories was subjective, but consideration was given to the qualifications of authors (eg whether they were members of the IFA) and whether they or their organisations appeared on the lists of archaeological consultants and contractors known to be involved in the preparation of desk-based assessments and field evaluations. Fig 44 presents an analysis of the results. From these it is clear that the proportion of reports dealing with archaeology prepared by qualified archaeologists has risen above 40% only in the last two years, and even then only to 60% in the South in 1990 and c 70% in the North in 1991. These findings carry two main implications. Firstly, the level of competence

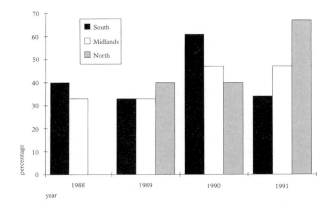

Fig 44 Percentage of archaeological elements in recorded environmental statements carried out by recognised archaeological contractors, sample size 145

brought to bear on the analysis and interpretation of the archaeological data reported in a high proportion of environmental statements is rather less than is appropriate given the nature of the studies involved. Secondly, archaeological organisations and professionally qualified practitioners do not appear to be heavily involved in the only area of assessment in the broad sense which has a statutory basis.

Funding and costs

No data were collected on the cost of preparing the archaeological elements of an environmental assessment, although they are believed to be about the same as for a desk-based assessment and field evaluation combined (Wood and Jones 1991, 28).

The nature of the report

Environmental assessment programmes are reported in the form of an environmental statement. This is typically a multi-volume report with a non-technical summary, a main statement, and a series of technical appendices. Environmental statements vary considerably in size and quality. The thickest are not necessarily the best and many lack sections which competently synthesise data and present conclusions in an accessible way. When environmental statements are available for purchase they are generally expensive (typically £100–£300).

As with other kinds of assessment report, few find their way into academic libraries. Major national collections have been established at the Environmental Assessment Centre, Manchester University, which collects a sample of those published each year (<25%), at the Impacts Assessment Unit of Oxford Brookes University, and at the Institute of Environmental Assessment. None of these collections possesses a complete set of statements published to date, although more or less complete lists of statements have been published in the *Journal of Planning and Environmental Law* and in directory form (Heaney and Therivel 1993). There is no national repository of all planning environmental statements, although the regulations require the submission of 'monitoring forms' and a copy of the statement itself (Wood and Jones 1991, 41).

The archaeological section is rarely a very substantial element of an environmental statement. One exception is the environmental state mentissued by English Heritage and the National Trust for the Stonehenge Conservation and Management Project (Darvill 1990).

7 Conclusions

Predictive studies

The survey presented in this report showed that over the last decade there has been a rapid growth in the number and scope of assessment exercises of all types. This is a considerable achievement of which the archaeological profession can be proud, especially given the relatively low starting position from which this growth has been reached and the speed with which approaches, methodologies, and procedures have been developed and tested. Indeed, in the 18 months since the end of the study period further growth has been evident and some of the early problems have been resolved. During data collection it became apparent that the rate of growth already described (Chapter 5, Desk-based assessments, How many, where, and when, and Field evaluations, How many, where, and when) continued into 1992.

Projections based on the figures collected in this survey are necessarily tentative, since the long-term influence of PPG 16 is still uncertain, the effects of recession unclear, and the level of consciousness about archaeological conservation still changing. At present, there does not appear to be a consistent relationship between the total number of planning applications and the proportion evaluated (see Fig 45). However, it seems likely that at some point the rising number of desk-based assessments and field evaluations will reach a ceiling, at which point a consistent relationship will become apparent. The introduction of PPG 16 towards the end of the period covered by this survey, at a time when about 0.12% of all planning applications were being evaluated, makes it particularly difficult to predict where this ceiling lies.

Fig 46a shows the actual rise in the number of desk-based assessments from 1988 to 1991 with projections forward to 1995 based on a number of predictions, a continuance of the trend visible in the evidence relating to the period 1988–91, the trend established by PPG 16 (modelled from data for November 1990–91), and the trend in place before PPG 16 was introduced (modelled from data for 1988–November 1990). It is apparent that even without the introduction of PPG 16 the rise in the level of desk-based assessments was likely to be considerable. Since the three models present such closely aligned results it is possible to argue that PPG 16 has had no significant effect on the level of desk-based assessment projects undertaken. A more important contributory factor may be the growth in

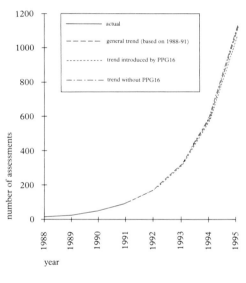

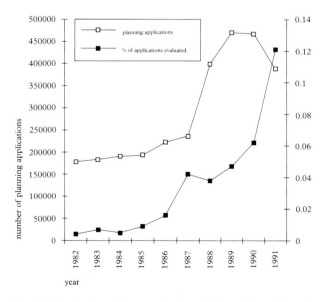

Fig 45 Total planning applications (left scale) against the percentage of those evaluated (right scale)

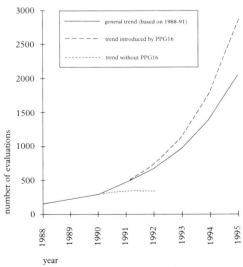

Fig 46 Predictive studies in the growth rates of assessment projects: (top) desk-based studies, (bottom) field evaluations

curator and developer confidence in the value of the desk-based study (see Chapter 5, Desk-based assessments, How many, where, and when, and The integration of desk-based assessments and field evaluations; also Pagoda Projects 1992). It has already been stated that the level at which a balance is reached in the ratio of planning applications to desk-based assessments is not at all clear, and may well be attained before 1995. However, there is no clear way of knowing at what point this will occur and no attempt has been made to predict it.

Predictive modelling from the current level of field evaluations was attempted using the same criteria as for desk-based assessments, but a very different range of outcomes resulted. In the projection for the level of field evaluations without the introduction of PPG 16 it is apparent that the rise in the number of field evaluations per year was already beginning to slow and would probably have reached a ceiling at about 380 projects a year. As the data for 1988–90 on Fig 46b show, this was not related to a stabilising of the percentage of planning applications evaluated and it therefore seems fair to assume that some other unidentified factor was at work in slowing the rise in the number of field evaluations. In the new situation introduced by PPG 16 this factor was removed and a substantial level of growth resulted (about 57% increase from 1990–91).

The forward projection of this growth rate suggests that in 1995 around 2500 field evaluations may be carried out if the ceiling in the ratio of planning applications to field evaluations has not been reached before then. A more modest forecast is based on a percentage rise in the number of field evaluations using figures for 1988–91 (average = 44%). At around 1900 projects this still represents a substantial increase in workload for all branches of the archaeological profession, and in particular in the workloads of archaeological curators and their assistants. In the early years of the decade under review a single officer was expected to deal with all the casework from his/her area, usually a county. In the ten years or so since that time the number of planning applications screened has doubled in most areas and the number of detailed appraisals carried out has increased nearly ten-fold in some areas. There has been no commensurate increase in staff levels. The policy and resource implications of rising numbers of desk-based studies and field evaluations for both SMRs and the NMR need to be considered.

Regional variations

The project revealed a considerable degree of regional variation in the ways in which assessment procedures are understood, designed, and implemented. This may be explained in part by differing local interpretations of PPG 16, which was still a relatively new document at the time of the study. Indeed, the whole business of assessment was, and still is, in its infancy. This cannot,

however, account for all the variation that can be seen. It is concluded from the analyses presented above that a great deal of regional variation is caused by the inconsistent application of judgement criteria and by localised interpretations of significance. It is important for the archaeological profession and for the sake of nationwide consistency that, even if the details of archaeology's place in the planning process vary throughout England, the process of interpretation should be standardised and should be seen to be based on more than intuitive judgement.

Methodologies

The techniques and methodologies used in assessment, and particularly those used in field evaluations, were developed for research rather than for the practicalities of archaeological resource management. Moreover, very little evidence was recorded which suggested that the techniques used were deployed in a way that took advantage of sampling theory. In some of the reports examined the strategy adopted appeared to be based on doing more and more work until something came to light. This cannot be justified in terms of the way in which professional judgement is normally exercised. A concomitant of making professional judgements is that sometimes the judgement will be wrong (ie a false positive or false negative). This has to be accepted as a fact of professional life, although within the profession as a whole a careful watch should be kept on the level of false positives and false negatives that can be recognised (through subsequent monitoring of approved developments) so that they can be kept to an acceptable level.

Assessment programmes need clear method statements which should then be adhered to. Staging the programme carefully greatly reduces the need for changes to the basic strategy. Careful selection of appropriate methodologies suited to the purpose of the programme is essential. The possibility of disjunction between the methodologies applied and the kinds of results expected from assessment programmes was identified as an important issue, for example in balancing the implications of information derived from different (sometimes complementary) techniques, and linking the results from different techniques with the application of the DoE's criteria of national importance. This is an area requiring further research at theoretical and empirical levels.

Reporting and publication

The preparation of reports on assessment programmes for clients has reached a high standard with the widespread availability of desk-top publishing systems and high-quality copying and mapping devices. However, the circulation and availability of such reports, or of summaries of the results of assessment programmes, are very poor. This has two main consequences. Firstly, the opportunities for informal peer review of work are minimal, because other members of the archaeological profession are seldom able to see either good or bad examples of work by others. Secondly, archaeological information is rendered inaccessible. The volume of information is also a problem. The quantity of reports now available is considerable and there is little in the way of standardised indexing or referencing systems.

The survey found that many assessment reports lacked the sort of basic information that would make cataloguing and indexing easy. It was found that when copies of reports were deposited in public records they were often filed in a manner that made retrieval difficult. Improving retrieval and accessibility will require a consolidated effort, and may be most easily brought about by professionally accepted good practice and peer pressure. A starting point would be the notification of assessment reports to *British Archaeological Bibliography* for listing alongside other kinds of reports and publications. In the longer term thought might be given to the creation of some kind of national agency to compile an annual gazetteer of desk-based archaeological assessments, field evaluation reports, and archaeological components of environmental statements.

Training and research

Assessment practices are still in their infancy and even relatively recent graduates will have had neither formal training in the subject nor the chance for critical reflection on methodologies or underpinning philosophies. This has two implications. First, relatively little original thinking has gone into the production of reports. Formats and templates have been carried over from job to job and perhaps on occasion even copied from work done by other organisations. In some cases the authors of different kinds of assessment report appear to have a poor understanding of why certain sets of information are included and how the consumers of the reports will use what is presented. Second, 'learning on the job' is both wasteful of resources and unfair to those on the receiving end of the services provided. If the number of assessment programmes undertaken continues to increase as suggested in the section on predictive studies in this chapter, then the need for fully trained staff who are both competent and experienced in all kinds of assessment will be very considerable. In addition, the techniques and procedures available to them at present will require tuning and reappraisal.

Many of the techniques used, in field evaluation in particular, have been carried over from academically-oriented research exercises. Although such techniques are useful for assessment projects they have limitations which are related to time/cost/ease of application, nature of land use, and the scale of the areas for which detailed knowledge is required. There is a need to appraise critically the techniques already in use in terms of their ability to deliver true results and to look at optimum combinations of different techniques for specific applications. There is also scope for the researching, testing, and development of new extensive survey techniques which have direct applications in field evaluation but are free of the constraints which apply to other techniques. Such new techniques would undoubtedly find a role in other types of archaeological work.

Records and review

The assessment process is a complicated one, involving a series of different stages (appraisal, desk-based assessment, field evaluation, etc) which variously correspond with key stages in the life-cycle of a development proposal or planning application (see Darvill and Gerrard 1994, fig 58, for summary). There are fine balances to be struck in the demands made upon applicants for further information. The survey revealed that so far there have been no serious challenges to the briefs and specifications issued by curators. It is, however, only a matter of time before such challenges are issued. For this reason it is appropriate that best practice should be periodically recorded and reviewed, a process begun in London (English Heritage 1992a–c) and developed through ACAO's model briefs and specifications (1993) and the IFA's work on draft standards in archaeology (IFA 1993a and b). Over the ten years reviewed by this project there have been many changes in the ways in which assessment programmes were conceived, planned, and implemented. Assessment is now a fact of life in archaeological resource management, although the parameters bounding its execution and its context in the planning system will no doubt continue to change. This process requires regular monitoring so that the correct levels of resourcing can be put in place and the relevance of procedures assured.

Professional matters

Assessment of all kinds requires considerable professional skill and the careful deployment of judgements. Because it involves decision-making it is important that records are kept of decisions and the reasoning underpinning them. The survey suggested that although considerable advances had been made in this sphere in recent years as archaeologists adjusted to the changing climate of work there was still room for improvement. This was especially notable with reference to reviews of work, communication between various parts of the profession, and the absence of method statements and source lists from desk-based assessment reports.

It is also a matter of some concern that archaeological contractors and consultants are not more frequently involved in the production of the archaeological components of environmental statements. It seems to be widely believed in some quarters that archaeological matters do not require specialist interpretation and professional guidance. This is a perception that the profession should take steps to change.

Optimising the results of assessment exercises is a matter for widespread professional concern. Assessment exercises are sometimes criticised for producing fragmentary evidence that makes no real contribution to the knowledge base of archaeology. In some senses this is true and can be directly linked with the restricted objectives of the assessment process (ie to provide information for decision-making). By the same token, however, the criticism also reflects a reluctance to grasp a new opportunity. The role of the curator is crucial in ensuring that the assessment process makes its contribution to archaeology locally, regionally, and nationally. This is potentially one of the most exciting challenges in archaeology this century.

As a result of this survey, the benefits of the assessment process can be seen at a number of different levels, two of which can be recognised as being particularly important.

Firstly, the revision of the basic data-sets on which archaeological inference and knowledge are based will be achieved mainly through the development process within the medium-term future. Desk-based archaeological assessments as the first level of response to a development proposal represent an input of time, skill, and experience for defined geographical areas at a level far in excess of what has been possible for most parts of the country to date. This effort needs to be channelled into the upgrading, enhancement, and validation of the basic index-level record that has been created so far. GIS technology and digital data handling make the mechanics of the task relatively easy, although the effective use of such technologies requires research and development so that workable, compatible, and archaeologically relevant systems are available. The costs and requirements of this kind of research and development are far in excess of what could reasonably be expected of a single county SMR and may better be carried out at a national level for the benefit of the profession as a whole. In this way, resources can be freed for deployment in the enhancement of records for areas where development is less intensive.

At a second, altogether different, level field evaluation can make a real academic contribution by changing expectations. Rather than hoping that something interesting will emerge from the work, a practical role for field evaluation can be developed through model-building and testing working propositions. In this way, pieces of data (whether positive or negative) from field evaluations would contribute to the resolution of problems and questions. The key is the development of good models and testable propositions. Here again the local or regional curator is of critical importance, because he/she is best placed to devise, or at least coordinate, these kinds of analyses. In the long term, the quality of the interpretations that can be made at the local and regional level will contribute to the ongoing development of the assessment process in that area and nationally.

Appendix 1
Archaeological
curators surveyed

The Assessment of Assessments project surveyed 97 offices in total, out of which the following list of curatorial offices were approached for specific data. All the curators of the following institutions were surveyed but not all were able to supply the required information in the time available. Fig 47 shows the geographical extent of the areas supported by complete or near-complete data. The institutions are listed in alphabetical, county order.

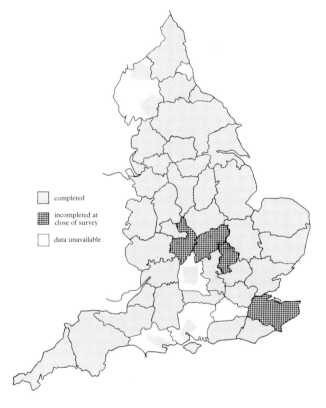

completed

incompleted at close of survey

data unavailable

Fig 47 Data capture from curatorial offices

Avon
Avon County Council Archaeological Unit
Bristol City Council
Bath Archaeological Trust
Bristol Development Corporation

Bedfordshire
Bedfordshire County Council

Berkshire
Berkshire County Council

Buckinghamshire
Buckinghamshire County Museum

Cambridgeshire
Cambridgeshire County Council

Cheshire
Cheshire County Council Archaeology Section
Chester City Council

Cleveland
Cleveland County Council Archaeology Section

Cornwall
Cornwall Archaeological Unit

Cumbria
Carlisle Archaeological Unit
Lake District National Park

Derbyshire
Derbyshire County Council
Peak District National Park

Devon
Devon County Council
Dartmoor National Park

Dorset
Dorset County Council
Poole Museum Service Archaeological Unit

Durham
Durham County Council

East Sussex
East Sussex County Council

Essex
Essex County Council

Gloucestershire
Gloucestershire County Council Archaeology Section
Gloucester City Council
The National Trust

Greater London
Museum of London Archaeology Service
Passmore Edwards Museum
Corporation of London

Greater Manchester
Greater Manchester Archaeological Unit
Trafford Park Development Corporation

Hampshire
Hampshire County Council
Winchester City Council
Southampton City Council Heritage Policy Section

Hereford and Worcester
Hereford Archaeological Unit
Hereford and Worcester County Council
Worcester City Council

Hertfordshire
Hertfordshire County Council

Humberside
Humberside County Council Archaeology Unit

Isle of Wight
Isle of Wight County Council Archaeology Centre

Kent
Kent County Council

Lancashire
Lancaster University Archaeological Unit

Leicestershire
Leicestershire County Council
Lincolnshire
Boston Borough Council
Lincoln City Council
Lincolnshire County Council
North Kesteven District Council
South Kesteven District Council

Merseyside
Merseyside Development Corporation
National Museum of Merseyside Field Archaeology
Section

Norfolk
Norfolk Landscape Archaeology

North Yorkshire
North York Moors National Park
North Yorkshire County Council
The National Trust Yorkshire Region
York Archaeological Trust
Yorkshire Dales National Park

Northamptonshire
Northamptonshire County Council

Northumberland
Northumberland County Council
Northumberland National Park

Nottinghamshire
Nottinghamshire County Council

Oxfordshire
Oxford City Council
Oxfordshire County Council

Shropshire
Shropshire County Council

Somerset
Exmoor National Park
Somerset County Council

South Yorkshire
Sheffield Development Corporation
South Yorkshire Archaeology Service

Staffordshire
Stafford Borough Council
Staffordshire County Council
Stoke on Trent City Council

Suffolk
Suffolk Archaeological Unit

Surrey
Surrey County Council

Tyne and Wear
Tyne and Wear County Council

Warwickshire
Warwickshire County Council

West Midlands
Black Country Development Corporation
Coventry City Field Archaeology Unit
Dudley Metropolitan Borough Council
Sandwell Metropolitan Borough Council
West Midlands Joint Data Team

West Sussex
Chichester Excavation Unit
West Sussex County Council

West Yorkshire
Leeds Development Corporation
West Yorkshire Archaeology Service

Wiltshire
Wiltshire County Council

Appendix 2 Archaeological contractors and consultants surveyed

The following contractors and consultants were contacted during the project and contributed material to the survey. A number of organisations who were contacted but, for various reasons, were unable to contribute directly to the project are not included on this list. The listing is divided-up according to the means by which contributions were made. See Fig 48 for a geographical spread of the headquarters of organizations contacted by the project.

Self-selected material submitted by post

Alison Borthwick, consultant
Archaeological Research Consultants (Norwich)
Avon County Council Archaeology Section
Barnstaple Archaeological Trust
Bath Archaeological Trust
Bristol City Museum Field Archaeology Section
Central Archaeological Services
Chester City Council Archaeology Service
Chichester Archaeological Unit
Cleveland County Council Archaeology Section
Cotswold Archaeological Trust
Durham University: Archaeology Department
Essex County Council Archaeology Section
Gwynedd Archaeological Trust
Harlow Museum
Hereford City Archaeological Unit
Isle of Wight Archaeological Centre
Liverpool Museum Field Archaeology Unit
R.P.S. Clouston
Southampton City Council Heritage Policy Section
Stafford District Archaeological Unit
Stoke on Trent Museum Field Archaeology Unit
Suffolk Archaeological Unit
Thames Valley Archaeological Services
The Archaeological Practice: Newcastle University
The Joint Data Team

Visited by a member of the project Team

AC archaeology
Bedfordshire Archaeology Service
Birmingham University Field Archaeology Unit
Bournemouth University
Buckinghamshire County Museum Service
Cambridgeshire County Council Archaeology Section
Canterbury Archaeological Trust
Cornwall Archaeological Unit
Exeter Museums Field Archaeology Unit
Gloucester Museum Archaeology Unit

Fig 48 Archaeological contractors and consultants surveyed

Gloucestershire County Council Archaeology Section
Hereford and Worcester Archaeology Section
Heritage Lincolnshire
Hertfordshire Archaeological Trust
Humberside Archaeology Unit
Leicestershire Archaeological Unit
Lincoln City Archaeology Unit
Lindsey Archaeological Services
Norfolk Archaeological Unit
North Hertfordshire Museums Field Archaeology Section
Northern Archaeological Associates
Oxford Archaeological Unit
Poole Museum Archaeological Unit
Shropshire County Council Archaeology Section
South Eastern Archaeological Services (formerly the Institute of Field Archaeology, London)
St Albans Museums Field Department
Tempus Reparatum, Oxford
Timothy Darvill Archaeological Consultants
Trust for Thanet Archaeology
Trust for Wessex Archaeology
University of Lancaster Archaeological Unit
Warwickshire Museum Archaeological Unit
York Archaeological Trust

Contractors whose reports were accessed from SMR, journal or annual review entries

Cambridgeshire Archaeological Unit
Fenland Archaeological Trust
Hampshire Archaeology / Test Valley Archaeological Trust
Ironbridge Gorge Museum Archaeological Unit
Ivor Jones, consultant
Kent Archaeological Rescue Unit
L and R A Adkins
MAP Archaeological Consultancy

Peterborough Museum
Rhys Williams, consultant
South Yorkshire Archaeology Unit
West Yorkshire Archaeological Unit

Note: Environmental statements were accessed through the Institute of Environmental Assessments, Lincolnshire, which is currently compiling a nationwide database of completed environmental statements.

Bibliography

ACAO, 1993 *Model briefs and specifications for archaeological assessments and field evaluations*, Bedford

Benson, D, 1972 A sites and monuments record for the Oxford Region, *Oxoniensia*, 37, 226–37

Binford, L, 1964 A consideration of archaeological research design, *American Antiquity*, 129, 425–41

Brereton, S, and Lambrick, G, circulated typescript report 1990 *The yield of archaeological field evaluations: a survey of projects undertaken by the Oxford Archaeological Unit and Wessex Archaeology*, Oxford

Burrow, I C G (ed), 1985 *County archaeological records: progress and potential*, Taunton

Champion, T, Shennan, S, and Cuming, P, 1995 *Planning for the past: volume 3; decision-making and field methods in archaeological evaluation*, Southampton

Darvill, T, 1987 *Ancient monuments in the countryside: an archaeological management review*, English Heritage Archaeology Report 5, London

—(ed), 1990 *Stonehenge conservation and management project: environmental statement*, Vols 1–3, London

—1993 *Valuing Britain's archaeological resource* (Bournemouth University Inaugural Lecture), Bournemouth

Darvill, T, Burrow, S, and Wildgust, D, 1994 *The assessment gazetteer 1982–91*, British Archaeological Bibliography Supplement 1, York

Darvill, T and Gerrard, C, 1992 Evaluating archaeological sites: the Cotswold Archaeological Trust approach, *Cotswold Archaeological Trust Ltd Annual Review*, 2 (1990), 10–15

—1994 *Cirencester: town and landscape*, Cirencester

Darvill, T, Saunders, A, and Startin, B, 1987 A question of national importance: approaches to the evaluation of ancient monuments for the Monuments Protection Programme in England, *Antiquity* 61, 393–408

DoE, 1983 *Criteria for the selection of ancient monuments*, Press Notice 523, London

—1989 *Environmental assessment: a guide to the procedures*, London

—1990 *Planning Policy Guidance 16: Archaeology and planning*, London

English Heritage, 1992a *London region archaeological guidance paper 1: model brief for an archaeological assessment*, London

—1992b *London region archaeological guidance paper 2: model brief for an archaeological evaluation*, London

—1992c *London region archaeological guidance paper 5: archaeological assessment and evaluation reports (guidelines)*, London

—1995 *Planning for the past: volume 1; a review of archaeological assessment procedures in England, 1982–1991*, London

Heaney, D, and Therivel, R, 1993 *Directory of environmental statements 1988–1992*, Oxford

IAM, circulated typescript report 1984, *England's archaeological resource: a rapid quantification of the National Archaeological Resource and a comparison with the Schedule of Ancient Monuments*, London

IFA, 1993a *Draft standards and guidance for archaeological desk-based studies*, Birmingham

—1993b *Draft standards and guidance for archaeological field evaluations*, Birmingham

Lawson, A, 1993 The assessment of trunk road schemes, *The Field Archaeologist*, 18, 351–5

MAFF, 1982 *Agricultural statistics*, London

Pagoda Projects, circulated typescript report 1992 *An evaluation of the impact of PPG 16 on archaeology and planning*, London

Palmer, R, and Cox, C, 1993 *Uses of aerial photography in archaeological evaluations*, Institute of Field Archaeologists Technical Paper 12, Birmingham

Ralston, I and Thomas, R, 1993 *Environmental assessment and archaeology*, IFA Occasional Paper 5, Birmingham

RCHME, 1993 *Recording England's past: a review of national and local sites and monuments records in England*, London

Saunders, A D, 1983 A century of ancient monuments legislation 1882–1982, *Antiquaries Journal* 43, 11–33

Spoerry, P, 1992 *The structure and funding of British archaeology: the Rescue questionnaire 1990–1991*, Hertford

Startin, B, 1993 Assessment of field remains in *Archaeological resource management in the UK: an introduction* (eds J Hunter and I Ralston), 184–96, Stroud and Birmingham

Wainwright, G J, 1992 Archaeology and the Department of Transport, *Archaeology Review* 1991–2, 8–18

Webster, G, 1963 *Practical archaeology: an introduction to archaeological field-work and excavation*, London

Wheeler, R E M, 1954 *Archaeology from the earth*, Oxford

Wood, C and Jones, C, 1991 *Monitoring environmental assessments and planning*, London

Woolley, C L, 1930 *Digging up the past*, London